おとなのORIGAMI-BOOK

オリガミ様の
お江戸折り紙

十二支おりがみ

Oriental Zodiac Origami

Bilingual, in Japanese and English

講談社

はじめに Introduction

　年初めに「四方を拝み」、家族揃って「柳の箸」でお雑煮を食べる。そして一年の吉を願い「恵方まわり」を済ます。ほどなく「豆まき」がやって来て、あっという間に田植えの季節が始まる——稲作を中心とした農耕社会を営んできた日本人にとって、芽吹きの季節である春はひときわ待ち遠しいもの。古来、お正月とは、まさに"迎春"のお祝いを意味していました。
　そのお正月を賑やかに彩る縁起物といえば、今も昔も「十二支」の動物でしょう。陰陽五行説という古代中国の思想から生まれた十二支は、もともとは12ヵ月の呼称として考案され、暦の普及とともに人々の暮らしに浸透していきました。今ではめっきり出番も少なくなりましたが、2月「初午」にお稲荷さんを祭る、といった十二支ゆかりの風習は残されていて、私たちの暮らしに季節感を与えてくれているのです。
　新年、年賀状の絵柄や飾り物として登場する十二支は、めでたい雰囲気とともに、人々におだやかな歳月の流れを感じさせてくれます。この美しい風習に思いを巡らしながら、家族団欒のひととき、本書を囲んで皆さんで折り紙を楽しんでいただければ幸いです。

「ゆしまの小林」四代目　**小林一夫**

目次 Contents

はじめに Introduction	2
十二支おりがみ ラインナップ Oriental Zodiac Origami Lineup	4
"紙の国"日本の折り紙 Origami from Japan, the "Country of Paper"	10
オリガミ様流 十二支おりがみの楽しみ方 Make the Most of Your Oriental Zodiac Origami!	12
折り図の記号、基本の折り方 Basic Origami Folds and Symbols	14
24枚の江戸千代紙 解説付き 24 Sheets of Edo-Chiyogami Paper with Explanation	17
折り図 Instructions & Diagrams	65

この本の使い方
How to use this book.

● ミシン目で千代紙をカットし、p65からの折り図を見ながら折ってみましょう。
Remove the paper designs by tearing along the perforated line, and fold using the instructions and diagrams from p65 onward.

● ☆マークは、難易度のレベルを表しています。
Stars express the degree of difficulty.

> ★　　簡単！ easy
> ★★　やや簡単 intermediate
> ★★★ ちょっと難しい more difficult

● 「折り図の記号」や、複数の折り方に共通する「基本の折り方」は、p14〜16を参照してください。
See pp14-16 for an explanation of folding symbols and basic folds.

● この本の千代紙で折ったあとは、お好みの模様やさまざまな大きさの紙で折って楽しんでください。
After using the paper in this book, enjoy folding with your favorite paper.

子(ね) ★★
Rat
17

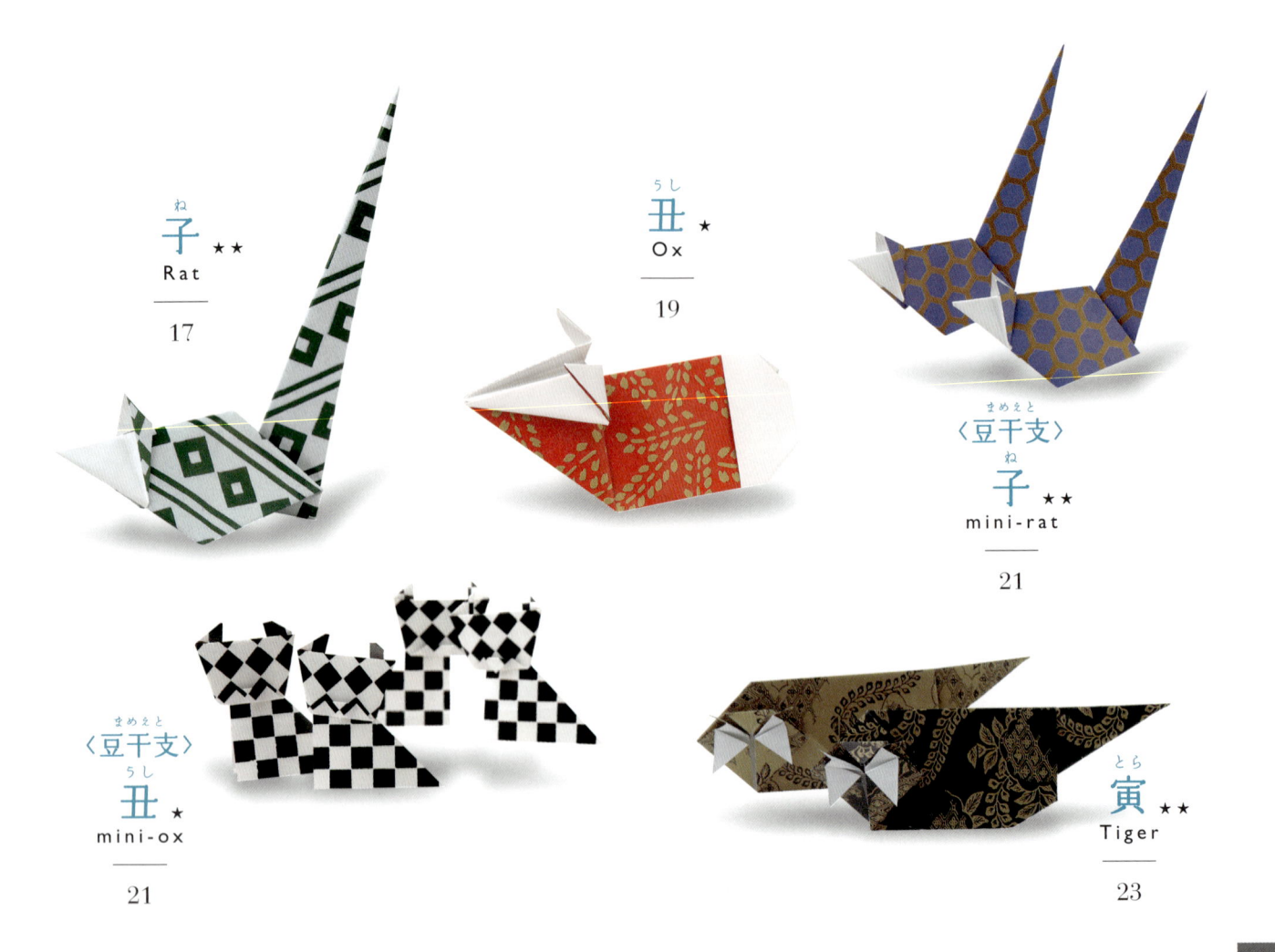

丑(うし) ★
Ox
19

〈豆干支(まめえと)〉
子(ね) ★★
mini-rat
21

〈豆干支(まめえと)〉
丑(うし) ★
mini-ox
21

寅(とら) ★★
Tiger
23

卯 ★
Rabbit
—
25

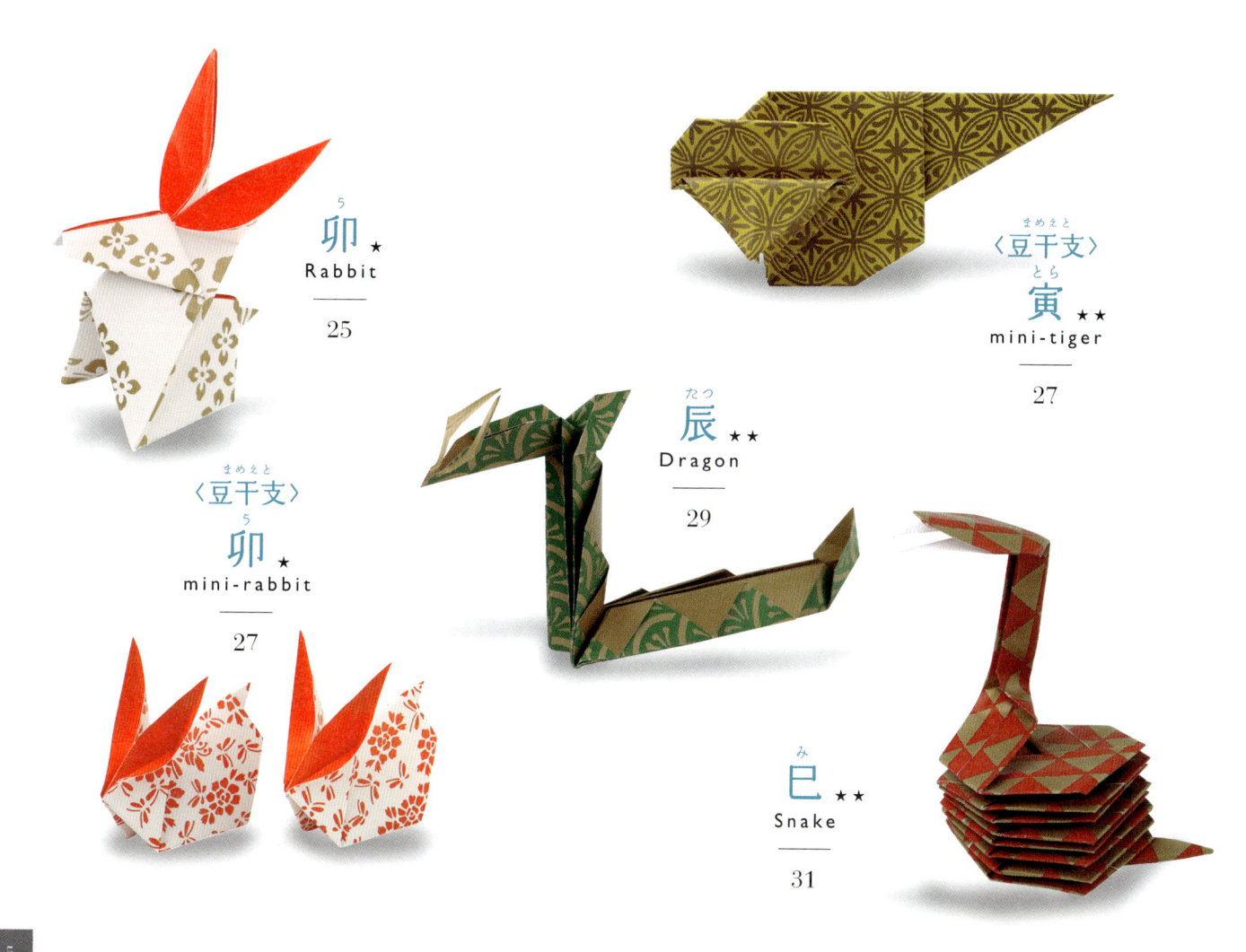

〈豆干支〉
寅 ★★
mini-tiger
—
27

〈豆干支〉
卯 ★
mini-rabbit
—
27

辰 ★★
Dragon
—
29

巳 ★★
Snake
—
31

〈豆干支〉
辰 ★★
mini-dragon
33

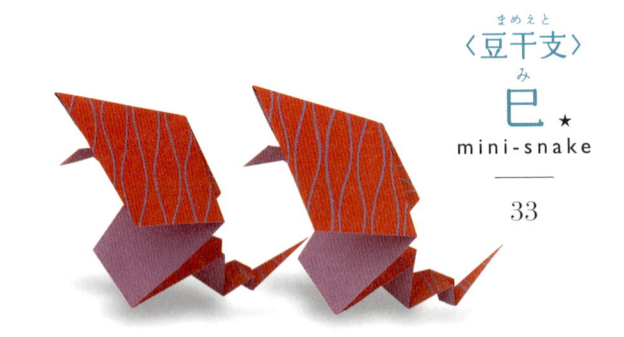

〈豆干支〉
巳 ★
mini-snake
33

午 ★
Horse
35

未 ★★★
Sheep
37

〈豆干支〉
午 ★★★
mini-horse
39

6

〈豆干支〉
未 ★
mini-sheep

39

申 ★★
Monkey

41

酉 ★★
Rooster

43

〈豆干支〉
申 ★★★
mini-monkey

45

〈豆干支〉
酉 ★
mini-rooster

45

戌 ★★
Dog
47

亥 ★★
Boar
49

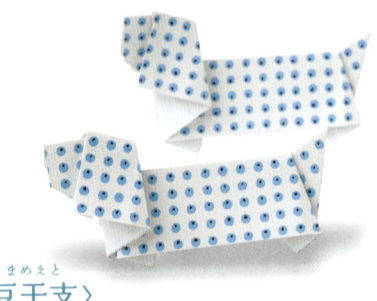

〈豆干支〉
戌 ★★★
mini-dog
51

〈豆干支〉
亥 ★
mini-boar
51

のしつき
ご祝儀袋 ★
Decorative envelope
with a noshi decoration
53

盃形の
お年玉袋 ★
Decorative
cup-style envelope
———
55

斜め帯の
お年玉袋 ★
Decorative envelope
with a sash
———
57

十文字の
ポチ袋 ★
Decorative envelope
with a cross
———
59

たとう折りの
ポチ袋 ★★
Tatō-ori
pochi-bukuro
———
61

伝承折りの
手紙 ★
Traditional
origami letter
———
63

"紙の国"日本の折り紙

小林一夫

　古代中国より伝わった紙。その後、日本では独自の紙漉き技術によって、より薄くて丈夫な紙が効率よく生産できるようになり、奈良時代にはすでに、各地で紙が作られていました。そして、日本の紙「和紙」とともに、「折り紙」の歴史も幕を開けました。

　折り紙といえば、「折り鶴」や「奴さん」といった遊戯折り紙を思い浮かべる方が多いでしょう。しかし、その起源は、古代、供物を神様に奉納する際などに、紙を折ったことにあると思われます。神社仏閣などにある御幣や紙垂などは、その名残でしょう。平安時代になると、贈物などを包む礼法「折り形」が多く生まれ、後世へと受け継がれていきました。遊びとしての折り紙が現れたのは、江戸時代のことでした。

　近年、ヨーロッパにも「折り鶴」や「奴さん」などと同じ形の折り紙作品があることから、「国が違っても人の発想は同じ」と考える折り紙愛好家が世界中に少なからずいるようです。しかし、私はそうは思いません。折り紙は、手から手へと伝え継がれてきた文化ですから、その起源についてはある程度は推察するほかありませんが、発祥の地が日本であることには、やはり疑いの余地がないと思います。

　例えば、折り紙がとても盛んな国スペイン。ヨーロッパにおける折り紙発祥の地といわれ、折り紙をスペイン独自の文化とする説もあるほどですが、私は今から約400年前にスペインを訪れた日本人使節団に注目しています。仙台藩主伊達政宗の命を受けた支倉常長ら「慶長遣欧使節団」です。彼らのうちの何人かはスペインに残り、現地の女性と結婚しているのです。折り紙は、その際に伝わったと見てもよいのではないでしょうか。スペイン折り紙協会のマーク「パハリータ（小鳥）」も、日本の伝承折り紙の「騙し舟」の変形と受け取ることもできるのです。

　古代日本人と神々の世界とを結んだ折り紙。「ORIGAMI」が国際語となった今、心を込めた一折りは世界中の人々をつないでいます。

Origami from Japan, the "Country of Paper"

Kazuo Kobayashi

Paper was originally introduced into Japan from China. The Japanese later developed new manufacturing techniques, resulting in paper that was both thinner and stronger. This came to be known as *washi* (Japanese paper), and was already being made all over the country by the Nara period (710–794). And with *washi* came the beginnings of *origami*, the art of paper folding.

For many people, the word "origami" probably brings to mind recreational paper folding to make such well-known figures as the crane or the kimono-clad Yakko-san. However, origami is thought to originate in votive offerings made from folded paper. The sacred staff with strips of paper attached (*gohei*) and the zigzag paper chains (*shide*) seen in Shinto shrines and Buddhist temples are probably vestiges of this practice. Also, many folding techniques derive from the *origata* of the Heian period (794–1185), when paper was used to wrap gifts. Recreational origami as we know it today dates from the Edo period (1603–1867).

Some European origami works have similar forms to the Japanese crane and Yakko-san figures, which seems to have led many origami enthusiasts around the world to conclude that people come up with the same ideas whatever country they are in. I beg to differ, however. Origami is a culture handed down from person to person, so to some extent one can only conjecture about its origins, but I really don't think there is doubt about it having originated in Japan.

Take Spain, where origami is really popular. Spain is said to be the birthplace of origami in Europe, and there are even theories that the art comes from its own culture—but what about that Japanese delegation that visited Spain around four hundred years ago? The Keichō Mission led by Hasekura Tsunenaga was a group of retainers of Date Masamune, the lord of Sendai, and a number of them married local girls and stayed behind in Spain. Isn't it possible that it was from them that the Spanish learned about origami? It is even conceivable that the *pajarita*—the "little bird" logo of the Spanish Association of Paper Folding (Asociación Española de Papiroflexia)—is derived from the traditional Japanese origami boat.

In ancient Japan, origami provided a link with the realm of the gods. Now that origami is an internationally recognized craft, a paper figure folded with feeling has the power to link people the world over.

オリガミ様流 十二支おりがみの楽しみ方
Make the Most of Your Oriental Zodiac Origami!

この本で折り上げた大小の十二支。さまざまにアレンジして、楽しみましょう。
Here Mr. Origami shares some ideas for displaying the origami figures in this book.

好みの台に飾り、お正月を演出
Make a traditional New Year's display!

敷板や塗りの盆、陶器のお皿など、好みの台に載せ、
玄関やリビングなどに飾ってみましょう。
お正月らしい雰囲気が演出できます。

Arrange the figures on a wooden board, lacquered tray,
ceramic plate, or other stand of your choice,
and display them in your entrance hall or living room
to create a typical New Year's mood.

バランスよい大きさの台を選びましょう。
Be sure to choose a stand that doesn't wobble!

豆干支シリーズの「巳」を
和紙のはがきに貼りました。
Here we attached a mini-snake
from our series to a *washi* postcard.

オリジナル年賀状を作る
Make your own New Year's cards!

市販の年賀状やポストカードに、
豆干支の折り紙を貼れば、
自分だけのオリジナル年賀状の完成です。

Affix mini oriental zodiac origami figures to
a shop-bought or homemade postcard to
make your own original New Year's greeting cards.

食卓を干支で飾る
Decorate your dinner table!

豆干支の折り紙は、箸置きとしても使えます。
また、箸袋に貼れば、かわいらしい祝箸になります。

The mini oriental zodiac origami figures can also be used as chopstick rests or as decoration for the chopstick sleeves to create a charming festive air.

うちわやお飾りにあしらう
Decorate fans and wreaths!

無地のうちわやお正月飾りなどに、
干支の折り紙をあしらえば、
日本情緒溢れるオーナメントになります。

Embellishing objects such as hand-held fans or small decorative wreaths with oriental zodiac origami figures will transform them into ornaments with a very Japanese flavor.

豆干支シリーズの「辰」を祝箸に。
Here we used the mini-dragon on chopstick sleeves.

うちわに大小の「酉」を貼り付けて。
Small and large roosters on a hand-held fan.

オリガミ様の道具箱
Mr. Origami's Toolbox

日々、新しい折り紙を生み出すオリガミ様。
折り紙をきれいに折るための
小道具を紹介します。

Mr. Origami dreams up new origami figures every day. Here he shares some tips on some of the essential items in his toolbox.

折り紙用ヘラ Spatula

美しい折りすじが楽につけられます。
木製のアイスクリームのさじや、ヘラ状のものでも代用できます。
This is the secret to making beautiful origami figures with crisp folds. Using a spatula makes light work of ensuring a clean and sharp fold.

医療用ピンセット Medical Tweezers

細かくて複雑な作品を折る際に活躍します。普通のピンセットでも代用できますが、医療用が使いやすいです。
These are really useful when making particularly tricky and complicated figures. You can use ordinary tweezers too, but medical tweezers are easier to use.

紙手芸用ボンド Paper Craft Glue

普通ののりよりも接着が早いのが特徴。
木工用ボンドでも代用できます。
This dries quicker than ordinary glues. You can also use woodworking glue.

折り図の記号
Origami Symbols

折り紙を折る前に、基本の折り図記号を覚えましょう。
これさえ覚えれば、折り図（p65〜）が簡単に理解できます。

Before starting on your origami, familiarizing yourself with these basic folds will make it easier to follow the instructions (which begin on page 65).

谷折り Valley fold

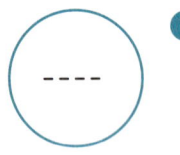

折ったあとの線が内側になるように折ります。
Fold the paper up to make an indented crease.

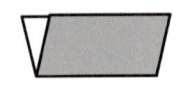

折りすじをつける Make a crease

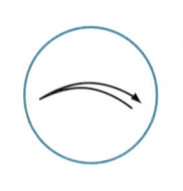

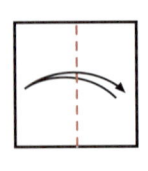

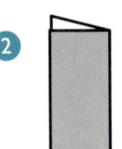

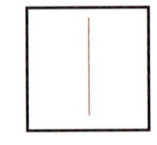

折ったあともどします。
Fold and unfold the paper to make a crease.

山折り Mountain fold

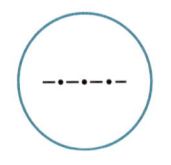

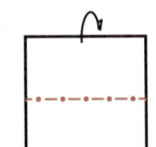

折ったあとの線が外側になるように折ります。
Fold the paper back to make a peak crease.

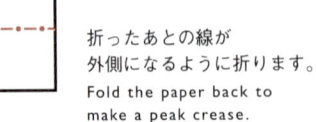

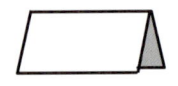

向きを変える Rotate

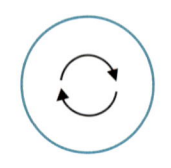

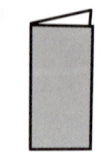

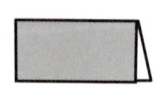

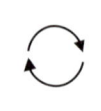

向きを変えます。
Turn as shown.

裏返す Turn the paper over

左右に裏返します。天地は変えません。
Flip the paper over to the left or right.
Do not turn round.

段折り Stair fold

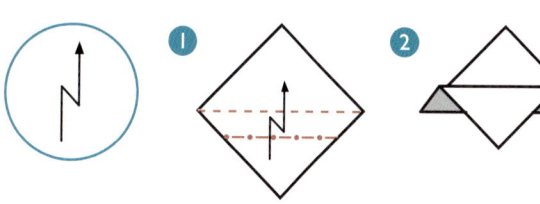

山折りと谷折りをして段にします。
Fold the paper using a mountain fold then a valley fold, like stairs.

図を拡大 Close-up

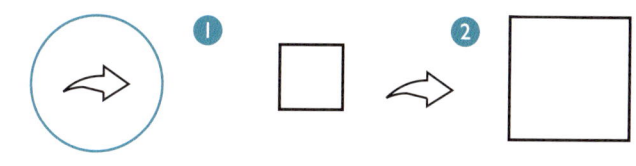

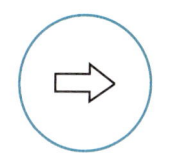

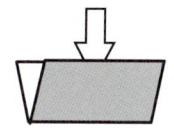

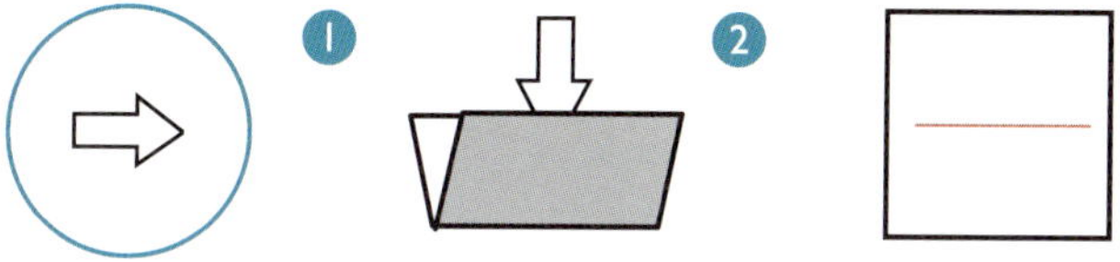

等分にする Divide

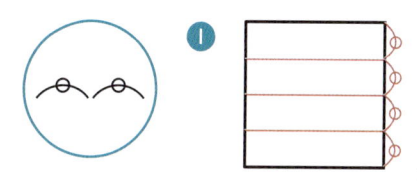

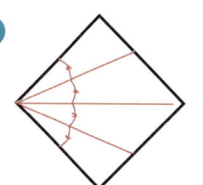

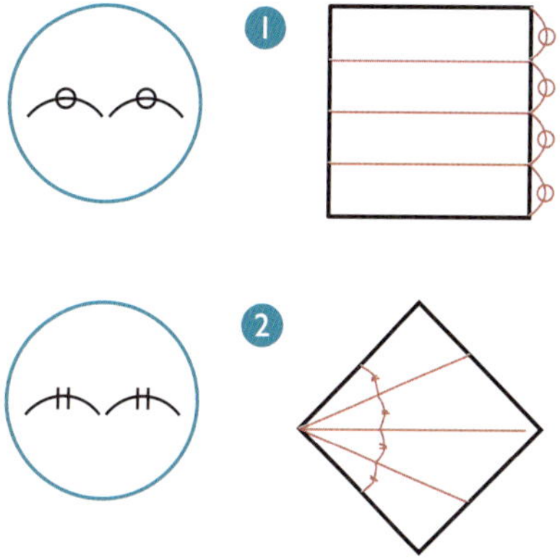

角度や辺を等分にします。
Divide the paper into equal sections of either the same width or angle.

あいだを開く Open up

基本の折り方
Basic Folds

いくつもの作品に共通する基本的な折り方です。
These basic folds are used in many figures.

三角折り Triangle box fold

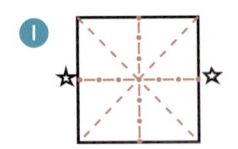

①
②

山折り、谷折りの折りすじをつけて、☆と☆がつくようにたたみます。
Make mountain and valley creases as shown.
Fit ☆ & ☆ together, folding the paper along the creases.

③ できあがり
Finished!

四角折り Square box fold

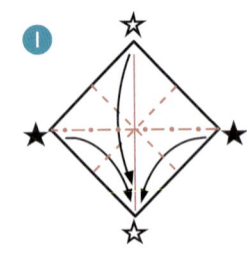

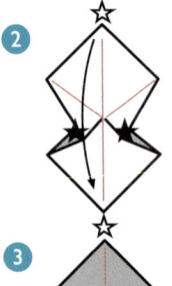

①
②

★と★、☆と☆がつくようにたたみます。
Fit ★&★ and ☆&☆ together, folding the paper along the creases.

山折りと谷折りをして折りすじをつけます。
Make mountain and valley creases as shown.

③ できあがり
Finished!

中割り折り Inside reverse fold

① 折りすじをつけます。
Make a crease.

② 内側に入れるように折ります。
Fold the tip inside along the crease.

③ できあがり
Finished!

かぶせ折り Outside reverse fold

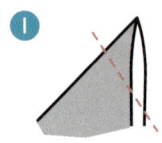

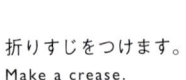

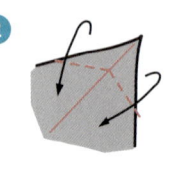

① 折りすじをつけます。
Make a crease.

② かぶせるように折ります。
Fold the tip outside along the crease.

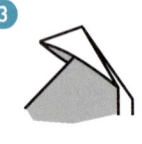

③ できあがり
Finished!

子
ね
Rat

子だくさんで、先を見通す力があるとされたねずみは古来、子宝・招福・蓄財の縁起物とされてきました。七福神の大黒天の使いでもあります。

Credited with many offspring and the power of foresight, the rat has been a lucky charm for fertility, good fortune, and prosperity since antiquity. It is also the companion of Daikoku, the god of wealth and one of the Seven Gods of Good Fortune.

→ 折り図 p65

賽の目つなぎ
さいのめつなぎ
Sainome Tsunagi

シンプルで粋な伝統文様。江戸時代から近代まで、祭り装束のたすきや帯などによく用いられました。子持ちの四角を、賽ころに見たててこう呼ばれます。

丑
うし
Ox

さまざまな地域で農耕神として崇められてきた牛。学問の神、天神さまの使いでもあり、赤べこは病気平癒にご利益があるとされています。

The ox is worshipped as the god of farming in many regions, and it is also the companion of Tenjin, the god of learning. The toy figure of a red cow called *akabeko* is thought to have the power to protect against sickness.

→ 折り図 p66

藤
Fuji

薄紫の房を揺らす美しい花姿が好まれ、古くから観賞されてきた藤。平安時代後期、藤原氏の盛栄とともに、公家の装束・調度に用いられる「有職文様」に取り入れられるようになりました。

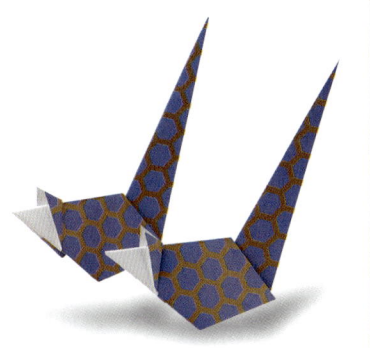

〈豆干支〉子
mini-rat ★★

→ 折り図 p67

〈豆干支〉丑
mini-ox ★

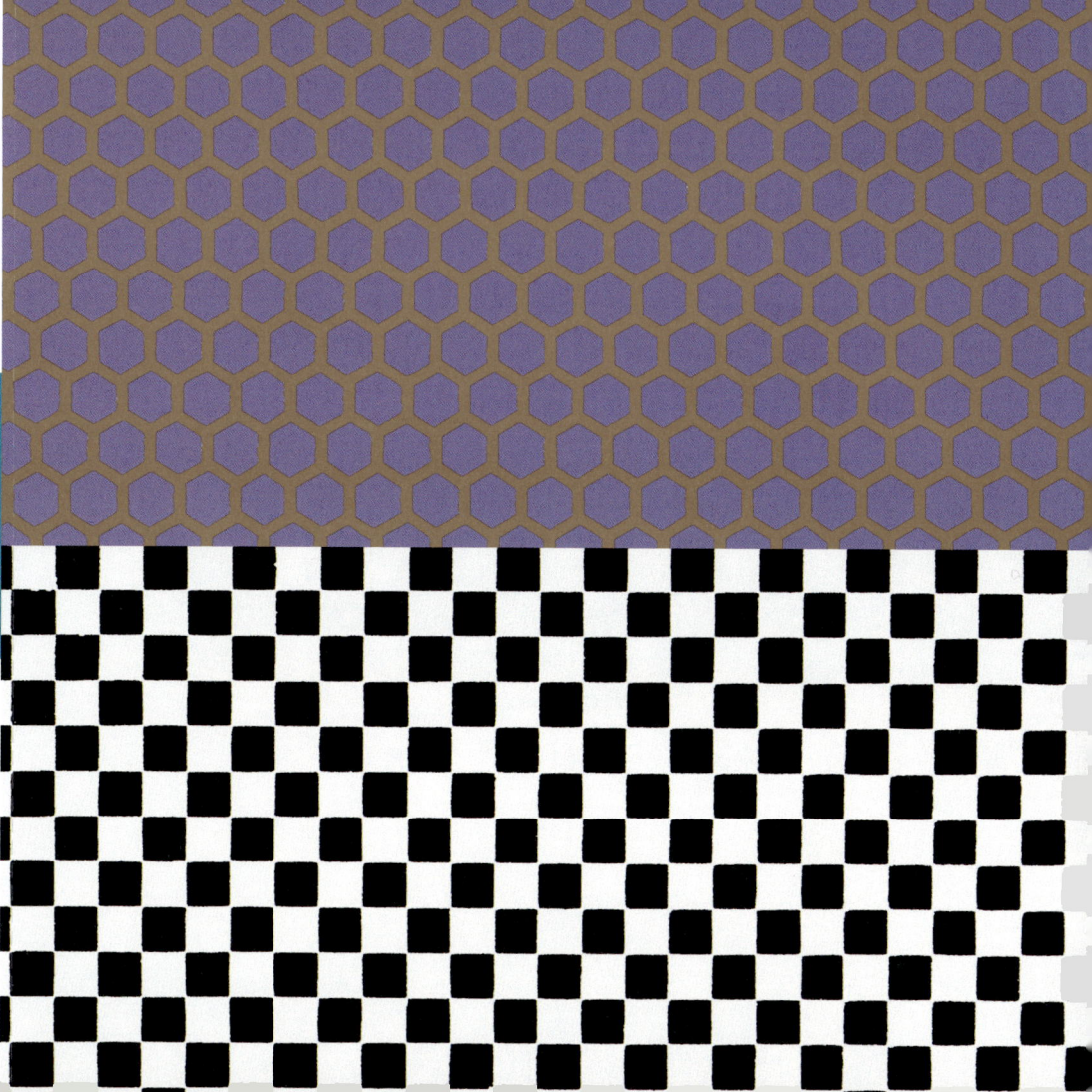

→ 折り図 p70

亀甲／市松
Kikkō/Ichimatsu

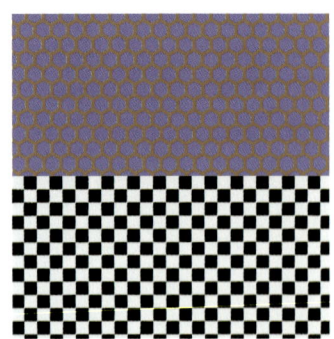

うす紫地の文様が「亀甲」。正六角形を亀の甲羅に見たてた「亀甲」は、古来、長寿を象徴する吉祥文とされてきました。
白と黒の文様が「市松」。古くは「石畳」と呼ばれていましたが、江戸時代に歌舞伎役者の佐野川市松が舞台衣装に用いて大流行して以降、「市松」文様と呼ばれるようになりました。

寅
とら
Tiger ★★

風水の四神のひとつ〈白虎(びゃっこ)〉として古くから知られていた虎。西の方角、あるいは玄関に飾れば、外からの邪気を祓(はら)ってくれます。一枚で、金と黒、2頭の虎ができます。

The tiger has been known since ancient times as Byakko, the White Tiger of the West, one of the four Taoist deities of feng shui. Hung in the west or in the entrance to your home, it will ward off external evil forces. With one sheet of paper you can make two tigers, one gold and one black.

→ 折り図 p68

<small>くもしっぽうつなぎとうか</small>
雲七宝つなぎ藤花
Kumo Shippō Tsunagi Tōka

格式の高い「有職文様」として、さまざまな図案に用いられてきた藤がゆるやかな曲線で描かれています。花房と葉のかたわらに、菱形のような「七宝つなぎ」を雲のなかに入れた意匠が配されています。

卯
Rabbit

うさぎを月と結びつけて考えるのは、世界的な現象のようです。日本でも月との関わりから、安産・子宝のお守りとされます。

Associating the rabbit with the moon seems to be a common phenomenon worldwide. This is also true of Japan, where it is a talisman for fertility and safe childbirth.

→ 折り図 p71

よつはなびし
四つ花菱
Yotsu Hanabishi

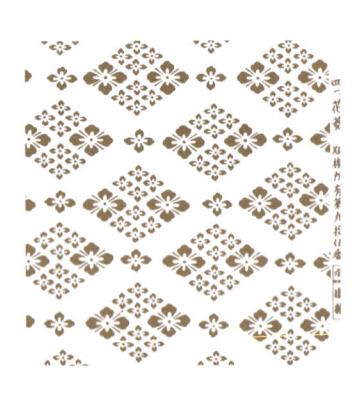

四弁の花を菱形に描いた文様は「花菱」と呼ばれ、平安時代には十二単や衣冠束帯に用いられるなど、とりわけ格式の高い文様とされていました。それを4つ集めてひとつの菱形にしたものが「四つ花菱」です。

→ 折り図 p72

〈豆干支〉寅
まめえと　とら
mini-tiger

〈豆干支〉卯
まめえと　う
mini-rabbit

→ 折り図 p73

花七宝／牡丹蝶
はなしっぽう／ぼたんちょう
Hana Shippō/Botan Chō

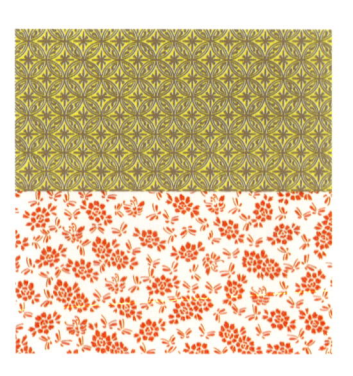

黄色地の文様が「花七宝」。同じ大きさの円の円周を四分の一ずつ重ねてつないでいく文様を「七宝」といい、その中心に花を入れたのが「花七宝」です。

白地の文様が「牡丹蝶」。花と蝶とを組み合わせた「花蝶文」のなかでも、中国で富貴の象徴とされた牡丹と、舞い遊ぶ蝶の姿との華やかな組み合わせはとりわけ好まれ、花札にも取り入れられました。

辰
Dragon
★★

中国では、四神のひとつ〈青龍〉として崇められてきた龍。邪気を祓う縁起物で、出世開運にもご利益があると考えられています。

In China, the dragon is venerated as the Blue Dragon of the East, one of the four Taoist deities. It is believed to ward off evil, and to answer prayers for success.

→ 折り図 p76

花青海波
はなせいがいは
Hana Seigaiha

同心の半円形を互い違いに重ねた「青海波」。古くは埴輪にもあしらわれましたが、波を表すものとして用いられるようになったのは、鎌倉時代以降とされています。円の代わりに花で「青海波」を形づくったのが「花青海波」です。

巳
み
Snake ★★

蛇は古くから水神の化身、あるいは使者と考えられていました。七福神の弁財天の使者で、技芸上達のお守りともされています。

Since ancient times the snake has been believed to be either the incarnation of the water god, or its messenger. It is also the messenger of Benzaiten, one of the Seven Gods of Good Fortune, and a talisman for proficiency in the arts.

→ 折り図 p74

うろこもん
鱗文
Urokomon

三角形を連ねた文様で、魚や蛇の鱗に似ていることから「鱗文」と呼ばれます。能や歌舞伎では、蛇に化身した女や鬼女がこの文様の着物を身につけます。近世では新撰組の制服の袖口などにも、用いられました。

→ 折り図 p77

〈豆干支〉**辰** ★★
まめえと　たつ
mini-dragon

〈豆干支〉**巳**
まめえと　み
mini-snake ★

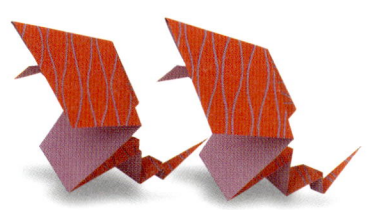

→ 折り図 p78

亀甲花菱／立涌
きっこうはなびし／たてわく
Kikkō Hanabishi/Tatewaku

黒地の文様が「亀甲花菱」。「亀甲」には多くの変形が見られますが、とりわけ好まれたのが、「亀甲」と「花菱」というふたつの有職文様を組み合わせたこの文様です。
赤地の文様が「立涌」。縦に走る波状の線が、水蒸気がゆらゆらと立ちのぼる様を表しているといわれます。代表的な有職文様のひとつです。

うま
午
Horse

神の乗物と考えられ、神聖視されてきた馬。2月の初午をはじめ、馬にまつわる年中行事は、今も日本各地に残っています。

As the mount of the gods, the horse is regarded as sacred. The start of the Year of the Horse in February is still heralded in parts of Japan with various events related to horses.

→ 折り図 p79

裏梅
うらうめ
Ura Ume

梅は奈良時代より少し前に中国から渡来したといわれ、その香りと花姿で王朝人を魅了しました。梅の花をモチーフにした文様は数多くありますが、「裏梅」は裏から見た花の形を図案化したもの。この千代紙には、横から見た梅の文様も配されています。

ひつじ
未
Sheep ★★★

キリスト教では、神に導かれる信徒にたとえられるひつじ。中国でも、神聖なものと考えられ、神への最高の供物のひとつとされていました。一枚で2頭のひつじができます。

In Christianity, the faithful are depicted as sheep led by Christ the shepherd. The sheep was also considered sacred in China, where it was one of the highest sacrificial offerings to the gods. With one sheet of paper you can make two sheep.

→ 折り図 p80

花の舞
はなのまい
Hana no Mai

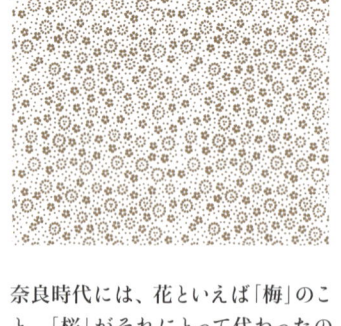

奈良時代には、花といえば「梅」のこと。「桜」がそれにとって代わったのは平安時代のことでした。以降、桜を意匠化して、数多くの文様が生まれました。「花の舞」は、満開の桜を思わせる華やかな文様です。

→ 折り図 p82

〈豆干支〉午
まめえと うま
mini-horse ★★★

〈豆干支〉未
まめえと ひつじ
mini-sheep ★

→ 折り図 p82

七宝花菱／観世水
しっぽうはなびし　　かんぜみず

Shippō Hanabishi/Kanze Mizu

青地に円形の模様が「七宝花菱」。「七宝」の円の中心に、「花菱」が配されています。七宝の円形は円満を表すとされ、古くから吉祥文とされてきました。
白地の文様が「観世水」。渦を巻いた水の文様で、能楽の観世家の定紋として用いられたことからこう呼ばれます。

申
さる
Monkey

★★

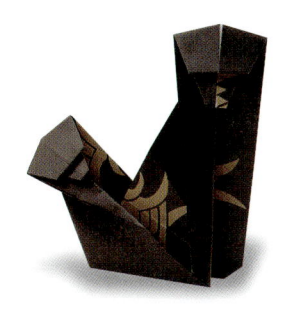

「悪いものが去る」の語呂あわせから、縁起のいい動物と考えられてきました。病気平癒や災難除けのお守りとしても知られています。

The Japanese word for monkey is *saru*, which is a homonym for the verb *saru* (to pass, depart), as in the phrase *warui mono ga saru*, or "bad things pass," and so the monkey came to be considered good luck. It is an amulet for recovery from illness and protection against disaster.

→ 折り図 p83

梵字
ぼんじ
Bonji

歌舞伎役者の名を配した「役者文様」など、文字を配する文様は数多くありますが、ここでモチーフとされているのは「梵字」。日本では、ひとつひとつの文字が諸仏諸尊を表す神聖な文字とされてきました。

酉 (とり)
Rooster ★★

甲高いひと啼きで朝を告げる鶏。古来、神の使いと考えられ、占いなどに用いられました。子どもの夜泣き封じにも霊験があるとされています。

> The rooster is the bird that announces daybreak with its shrill cry. In ancient times it was believed to be a messenger of the gods, and was used for telling fortunes. It is also believed to have the magical power to stop children crying at night.

→ 折り図 p84

扇面に小紋
せんめんにこもん
Senmen ni Komon

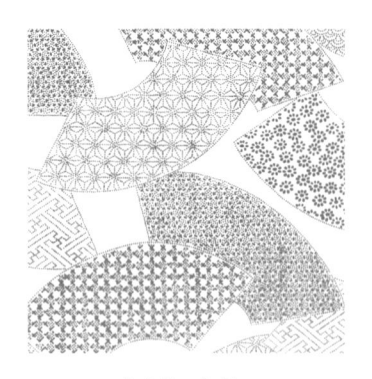

「麻の葉」「紗綾形」「亀甲」などの小紋が、扇形にして組み合わされています。「末広」とも呼ばれ、縁起物の代表格とされてきた扇子と、いくつもの吉祥文を合わせることで、めでたさを強調しています。

→ 折り図 p86

〈豆干支〉申
まめえと　さる
mini-monkey
★★★

〈豆干支〉酉
まめえと　とり
mini-rooster
★

→ 折り図 p87

蝶／翁格子
ちょう／おきなごうし
Chō/Okina Gōshi

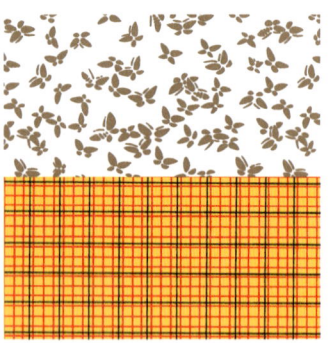

白地の文様が「蝶」。幼虫からサナギとなり、さらに羽化して飛び立つ蝶は、不死・不滅の象徴として考えられ、武家の紋などに好まれました。
黄色地の文様が「翁格子」。大きな格子の中に、多数の小さな格子を表したこの文様は、その様子を翁が大勢の孫子を持つことになぞらえ、子孫繁栄の意味をもつとされます。

戌
(いぬ)

Dog ★★

安産・子宝のお守りとして親しまれている犬。妊娠5ヵ月目に入った最初の戌の日に腹帯を巻き、安産祈願をするという風習は、今でも広く行われています。

The dog is beloved as a lucky charm for fertility and childbirth. Even today, many women follow the custom of wrapping a cloth band around their waists on the Day of the Dog to pray for a safe delivery.

→ 折り図 p88

丸紋尽くし
まるもんづくし
Marumon Zukushi

花や蝶、植物などをあしらったさまざまな家紋を並べた文様で、能や狂言、歌舞伎などの装束に用いられます。「道成寺」の白拍子をはじめ、魔的な要素を潜めた人物が、この文様の衣装を身につけます。

亥
Boar

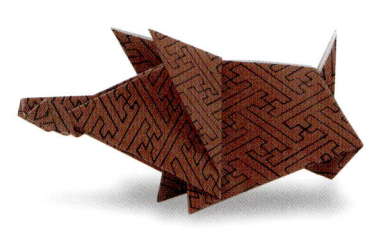

「猪突猛進」の言葉もあるように、猪は古来、勇気や武勇の象徴とされてきました。火を防ぐ動物ともいわれるので、家内安全のお守りにもなります。

The boar is sometimes considered reckless, but since antiquity it has been a symbol of bravery and valor. It is also said to protect against fire, and is a talisman for safety within the home.

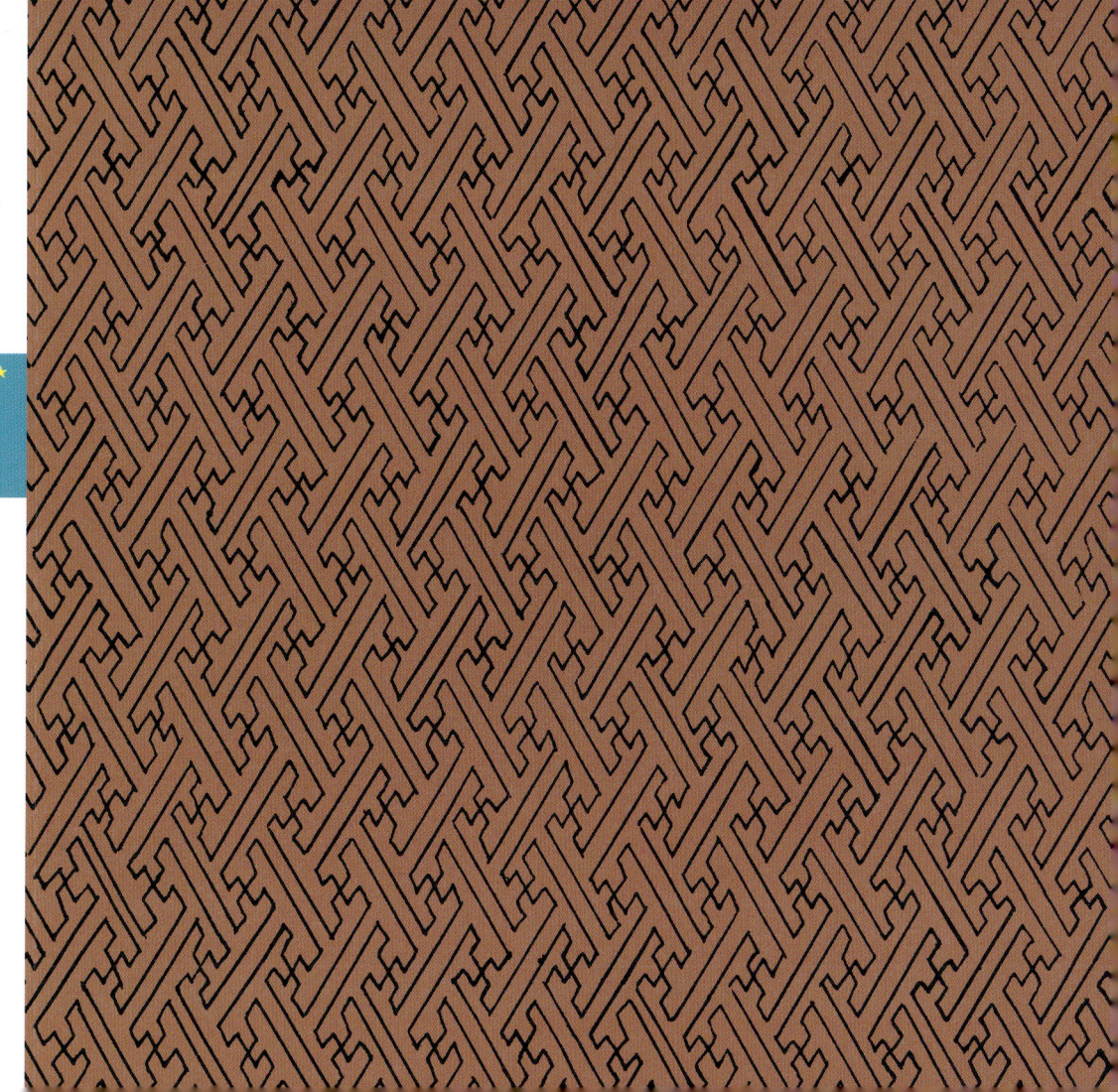

→ 折り図 p89

紗綾形
Sayagata

卍を斜めにつないだ連続文様で、「卍崩し」または「卍つなぎ」ともいいます。明時代の中国から伝わった絹織物「紗綾」の地紋として用いられたことから、こう呼ばれます。

〈豆干支〉**戌** ★★★
mini-dog

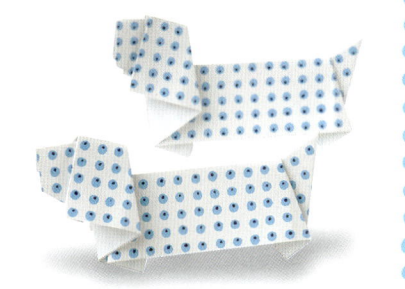

→ 折り図 p90

〈豆干支〉**亥** ★
mini-boar

→ 折り図 p91

豆絞り/五崩し
Mameshibori/Gokuzushi

白地の文様が「豆絞り」。江戸の庶民に親しまれた文様のひとつで、ひょっとこ踊りの頬かむりには、「豆絞り」の手拭いと決まっています。
紫地の文様が「五崩し」。棒が並んだところが、和算や易占に使う道具「算木」を崩した様を思わせることから「算木崩し」とも呼ばれます。三本ずつ縦横互い違いに配したものを「三崩し」、五本のものを「五崩し」といいます。

のしつきご祝儀袋
のしつきごしゅうぎぶくろ
Decorative envelope with a noshi decoration

お祝い事には欠かせない〈熨斗〉を折り込んだ伝承のご祝儀袋。日本には古来、包みの折り方にさまざまな決まり事を付した〈折り形〉という礼法があり、武家などの格式高い家に伝承されていました。

For celebratory occasions, money is gifted in a folded envelope decorated with a *noshi*, originally a strip of dried abalone. In olden times, various conventions governed how the paper should be folded, and some elite samurai families even had their own designs.

→ 折り図 p92

柳に燕
Yanagi ni Tsubame

尾羽をなびかせて軽やかに飛ぶ燕と、しなやかに伸びる柳の枝。この早春の風物詩の取り合わせは、江戸庶民のあいだでとりわけ人気があり、さまざまな文様が生まれました。

盃形のお年玉袋
さかずきがたのおとしだまぶくろ
Decorative cup-style envelope

おなじみの〈紙コップ〉の折り紙も千代紙で折れば、きれいなお年玉袋に。ボタンなどの小物をしまっておいてもよいでしょう。

Made with colorful chiyogami paper, the familiar origami paper cup can be transformed into a pretty envelope for *otoshidama*, the New Year's gift of money to a child. You can also use it to store buttons or other small objects.

→ 折り図 p93

縞に桐
しまにきり
Shima ni Kiri

中国で鳳凰の住む木として尊ばれた桐。日本では、足利氏や豊臣氏をはじめ、多くの武家の紋に用いられてきました。大正時代につくられたこの木版千代紙では、桐の花と縞が大胆に図案化されています。

ななめおびのおとしだまぶくろ
斜め帯のお年玉袋
Decorative envelope with a sash

お金を包む「折り形」のひとつで、さっと手軽に折れるのが魅力です。お年玉袋のほか、慶事などで心付けを渡す際に用いてもよいでしょう。

For this style of folded envelope used for gifts of money, the charm lies in being able to fold it quickly and simply. You can use it for New Year's *otoshidama*, or for any celebratory occasion.

→ 折り図 p93

朝顔
あさがお
Asagao

日本では夏になると、着物の柄に秋草を取り入れるなどして、涼を演出する風習があります。そんななか盛夏の花でありながら涼しげな印象があるとして好まれたのが、朝顔の文様。青竹の格子との組み合わせは、とりわけ清涼感があります。

十文字のポチ袋
Decorative envelope with a cross

真っ白な十文字が美しいポチ袋。関西では、芸妓さんにあげるチップのことを〈ポチ〉と言い、それを入れる包みが〈ポチ袋〉と呼ばれるようになりました。

A lovely gift envelope bearing the form of a pure white cross. In Kyoto, the tip paid to a geisha is called a *pochi*, and the envelope used for this tip came to be called a *pochi-bukuro*.

→ 折り図 p94

<small>はないしだたみ</small>
花石畳
Hana Ishidatami

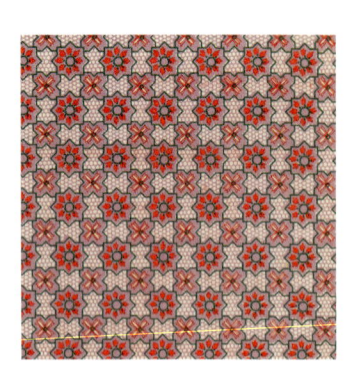

「花菱」や「花の舞」など、日本では古来、花を特定せずに意匠化した文様が数多くつくられてきました。ここでは、花を互い違いに石畳のように配し、そのあいだを小さな「亀甲」文様で埋めています。

たとう折りのポチ袋
Tatō-ori pochi-bukuro

たとうとは〈畳紙(たとうがみ)〉の略で、折り畳んで懐中する紙のことです。江戸時代には薬や糸くずなどを入れておくのに用いられましたが、ポチ袋にもぴったりです。

Tatō is an abbreviation of *tatōgami*, the folded paper pouch that was used for medicine or pieces of thread and so forth in the Edo period. It also makes an ideal *pochi-bukuro*.

→ 折り図 p95

枝梅
Eda Ume

松、竹と並ぶ吉祥文として親しまれてきた梅。古来、さまざまに意匠化されてきましたが、梅の花弁の文様を「梅花文」、花が枝についた文様を「枝梅」、そして梅の木全体の文様は「梅樹文」と呼ばれます。

伝承折りの手紙
でんしょうおりのてがみ
Traditional origami letter

伝承の「折り形」のひとつで、本来は粉包み。蝶の形をした美しい折りなので、贈り物に添えるメッセージカードなどに使えるよう、裏にケイ線を入れました。

One of the traditional folding methods originally used as a container for flour, this beautiful butterfly shape is also great as a gift card to accompany a present.

→ 折り図 p95

夜桜
よざくら
Yozakura

平安の昔から、日本人の心を捉えてきた桜ですが、その文様が庶民のものとなったのは江戸時代のことです。小さな花を一面に散らした「桜散らし」や「小桜」などの文様が、小紋柄として愛用されました。ここでは、艶やかな夜桜が表されています。

★★ 子 Rat → 折り紙 p17

折り図
Instructions & Diagrams

●「折り図の記号」や「基本の折り方」は、p14〜16を参照。紙はグレーの面が表です。
See pp14–16, for an explanation of folding symbols and basic folds.

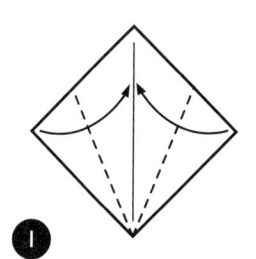

① 三角に折って折りすじをつけ、中央の線にあうように折ります。
Fold in half to form a triangle and make a crease, and then fold each side in to meet at the crease.

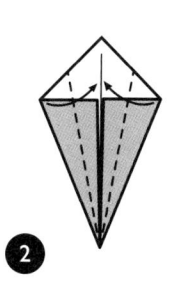

② さらに、折ります。
Fold in both sides once more.

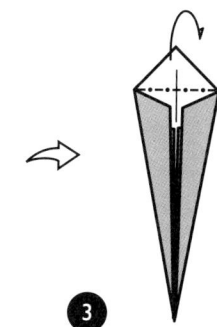

③ 図のように山折り。
Make a mountain fold as shown.

④ 角を中央にあわせるように折ります。
Fold the corners over to meet in the center.

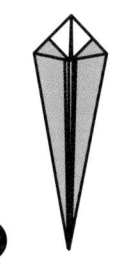

⑤ 折ったところ。
This is how it should look.

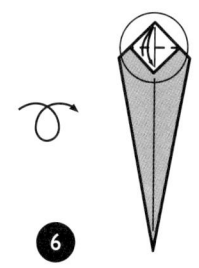

⑥ 折りすじをつけます。
Make a crease.

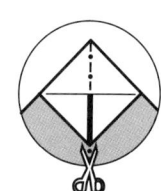

⑦ 半分位まで切り込みをいれてから、全体を半分に山折り。
Make a cut up to the crease, and then fold in half lengthwise using a mountain fold.

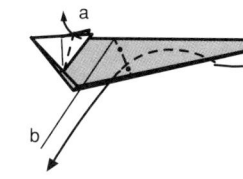

⑧ aを谷折りして耳を作ります。(裏も同様に) bの線にあわせるように「中割り折り」(→p16)。
On both sides, fold 〈a〉 using a valley fold to make the ears, and then make an inside reverse fold along line 〈b〉.

⑨ 折ったところ。尾を矢印の方向に「中割り折り」。
Make another inside reverse fold for the tail.

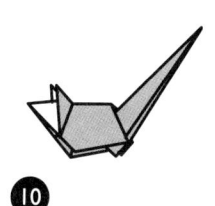

⑩ できあがり
Finished!

65

★

丑 ○x → 折り紙 p19

原案 ｜ 中島 進

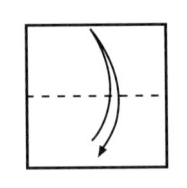

1. 半分に折って折りすじをつけます。
Fold in half and make a crease.

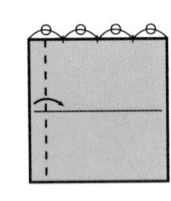

2. 1/4のところに印をつけ、そこにあわせて折ります。
Make a mark 1/4 way along the side, and fold over so the edge meets up with the mark.

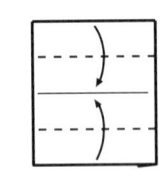

3. 1でつけた折りすじにあうように折ります。
Fold over so the edges meet at the crease made in step 1.

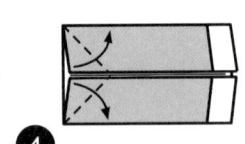

4. 角を2ヵ所折ります。
Fold the corners as shown.

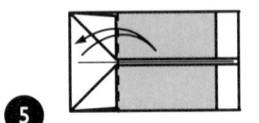

5. 折りすじをつけます。
Make a crease.

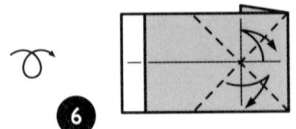

6. 折りすじをつけます。
Make creases.

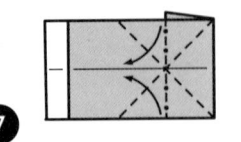

7. 折りすじを使って、「三角折り」（→p16）の要領で折ります。
Use the creases to make a triangular box fold.

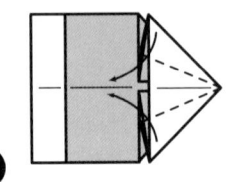

8. 上の1組をそれぞれ中央の線にあわせて折ります。
Fold the top flap over on each side to align at the center.

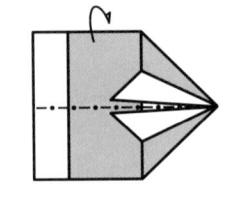

9. 全体を半分に山折り。
Fold in half using a mountain fold.

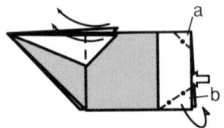

10. 角をそれぞれ谷折り。aは「中割り折り」（→p16）し、bはあいだを開いて内側に折り込みます。（裏も同様に）
Make valley folds on the corners of the triangle as shown. Make an inside reverse fold at ⟨a⟩, and fold in on each side at ⟨b⟩.

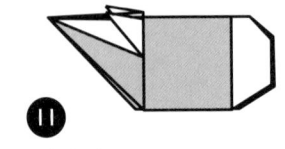

11. できあがり
Finished!

★★ 〈豆干支〉子 mini-rat → 折り紙 p21

注 千代紙「亀甲」(紫) を使用。裏の点線で切ってください。2匹のねずみができます。
Note: Use "Kikkō" chiyogami paper (purple). Cut along the dotted line on the back to make two mini-rats.

1 三角に切ります。
Cut to make two triangles as shown.

2 図のように折ります。
Fold as shown.

3 ☆と★があうように折って、折りすじをつけます。
Fold over so the two stars meet and make a crease.

4 3でつけた折りすじで2枚まとめて切り落とし、開きます。
Cut both sides together along the crease made in step 3.

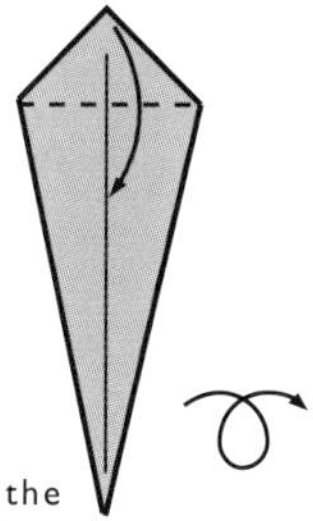

5 図のように折ります。
Fold over the top triangle as shown.

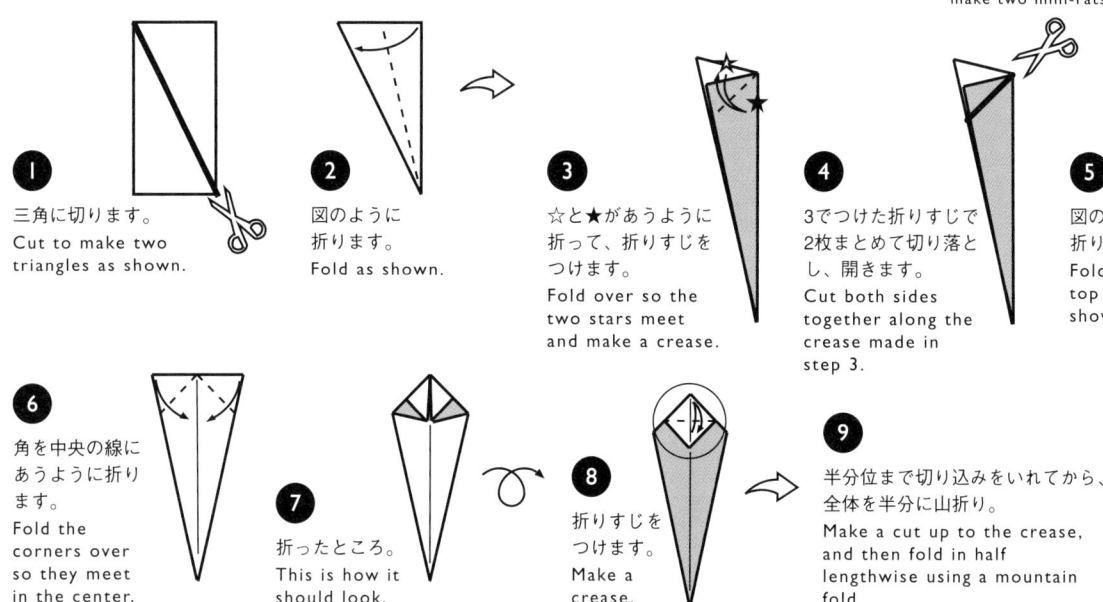

6 角を中央の線にあうように折ります。
Fold the corners over so they meet in the center.

7 折ったところ。
This is how it should look.

8 折りすじをつけます。
Make a crease.

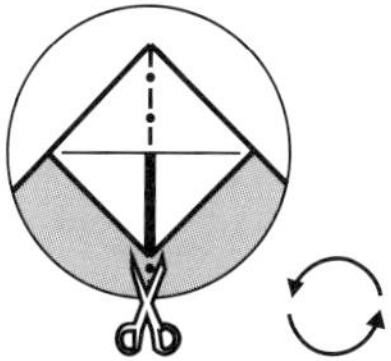

9 半分位まで切り込みをいれてから、全体を半分に山折り。
Make a cut up to the crease, and then fold in half lengthwise using a mountain fold.

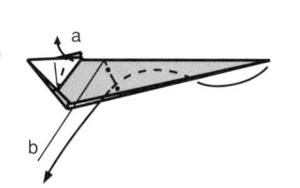

10 aを谷折りして耳を作ります。(裏も同様に) bの線にあわせるように「中割り折り」(→p16)。
On both sides, fold 〈a〉 using a valley fold to make the ears, and then make an inside reverse fold along line 〈b〉.

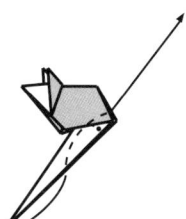

11 折ったところ。尾を矢印の方向に「中割り折り」。
Make another inside reverse fold to make a tail.

12 できあがり
Finished!

★★ 寅 Tiger → 折り紙 p23

注 千代紙を裏の点線で切ってください。
金と黒、2頭の虎ができます。
Note: Cut the chiyogami paper along the dotted line on the back to make two tigers, one gold and one black.

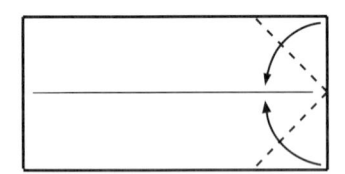

1
半分に折って折りすじをつけ、角を2ヵ所折ります。
Fold in half to make a crease, and then fold in two corners as shown.

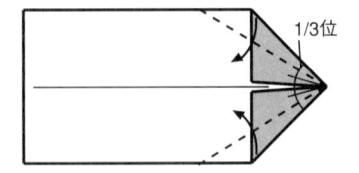

2
それぞれ、角の1/3位のところで折ります。
Fold the corners over again, this time by 1/3.

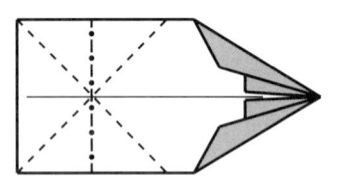

1/3位

3
折りすじをつけます。
Make creases.

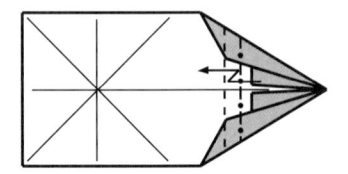

4
図の位置で段折りします。
Make a stair fold as shown.

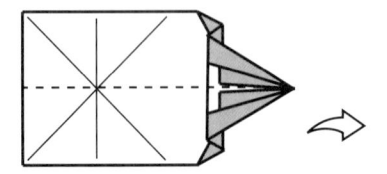

5
全体を半分に谷折り。
Fold in half using a valley fold.

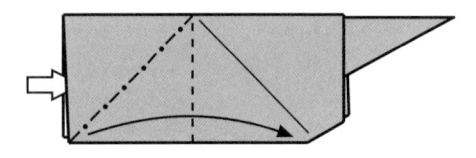

6
あいだを開いて、右に倒してたたみます。
Open out and fold over to the right as shown.

68

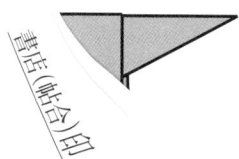

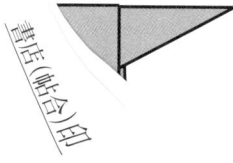

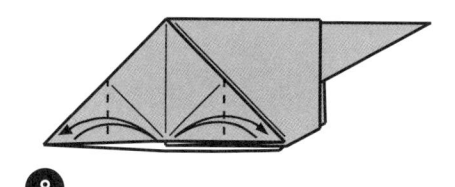

8
さらに折りすじをつけます。
Make further creases as shown.

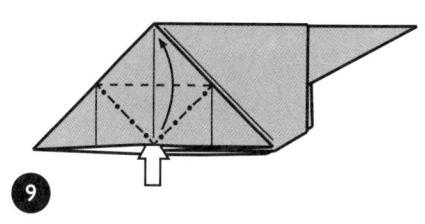

9
あいだを開いて、上に折り上げます。
Open out and fold upwards.

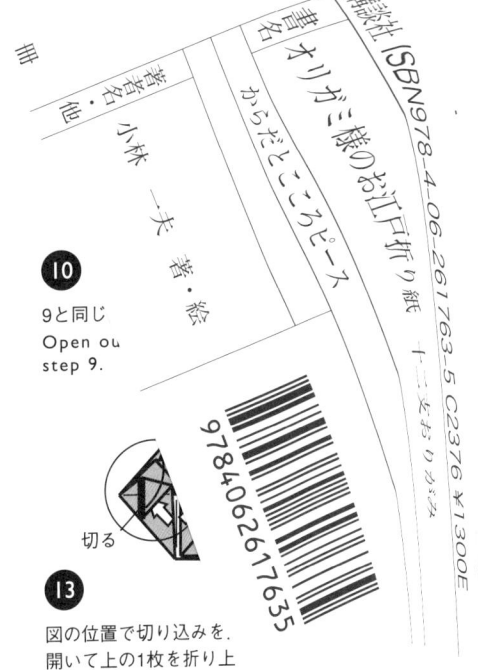

10
9と同じ
Open out step 9.

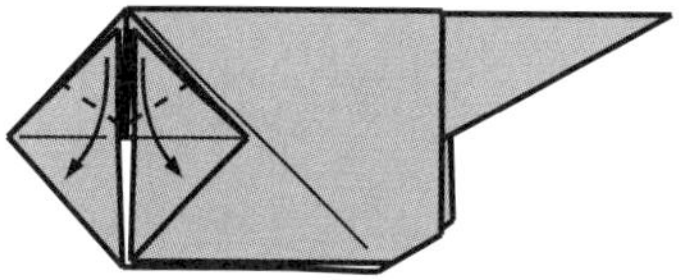

11
斜めに折ります。
Fold both flaps down at an angle.

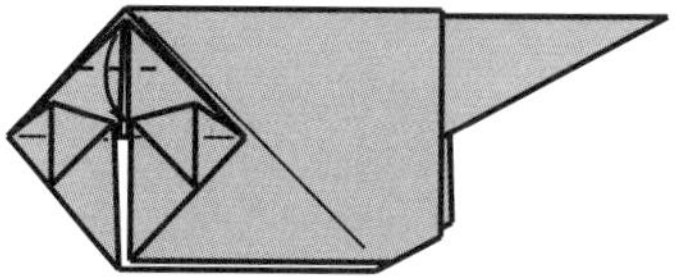

12
上の1枚を三角に折ります。
Fold the top triangle down as shown.

13
図の位置で切り込みを。
開いて上の1枚を折り上
Cut the flaps as shown...
up the top layers as sh...

切る

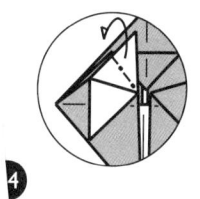

14
...分に山折り。
...d the top flap over by half using a mountain fold.

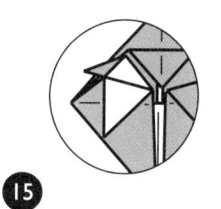

15
折ったところ。
（右側も同様に）
Repeat on the other side.

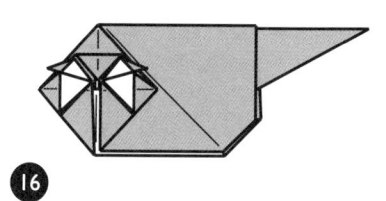

16
できあがり
Finished!

★ 〈豆干支〉丑 mini-ox → 折り紙 p21

注 千代紙「市松」(白・黒)を使用。裏の点線で8等分に切ってください。4頭の牛ができます。
Note: Use "Ichimatsu" chiyogami paper (black and white). Cut into 8 equal parts along the dotted lines on the back to make four mini-oxes.

体 Body

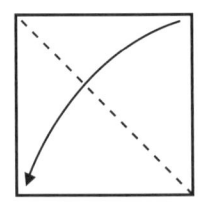

1 三角に折ります。
Fold over to make a triangle.

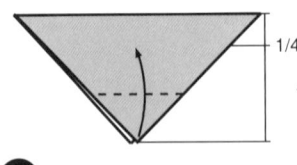

2 体のできあがり
That's the body finished!

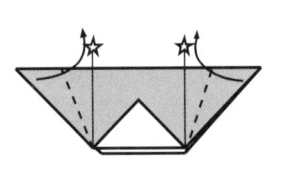

頭 Head

1 三角に折って、上の一枚のみ、上から1/4のところにあうように折ります。
Fold over to make a triangle and fold the top sheet only up to meet the 1/4 mark as shown.

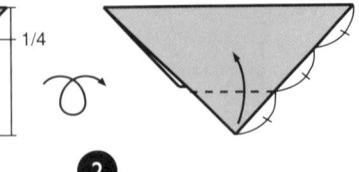

2 1/3のところで折ります。
Fold over the top third as shown.

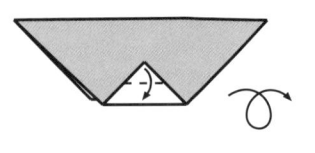

3 2で折ったところを半分に折ります。
Fold the flap made in step 2 in half.

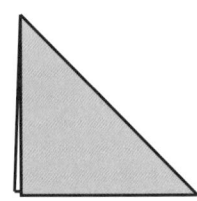

4 ☆の線にあうように両側を谷折り。
Fold each side using a valley fold so that they align with the stars as shown.

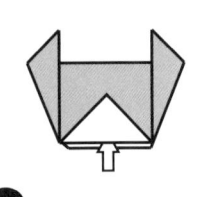

5 折ったところ。矢印部分に体を差し込みます。
Insert the body into the head as indicated with the arrow.

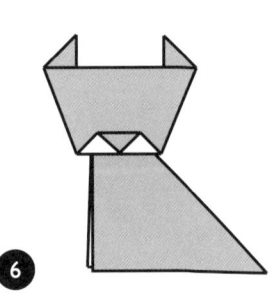

6 できあがり
Finished!

70

卯 Rabbit → 折り紙 p25

1. 「四角折り」(→p16) をして、図のように折りすじをつけます。
Make a square box fold, and then make creases as shown.

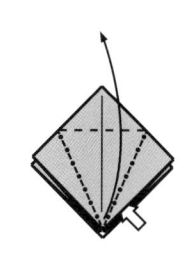

2. 上の1枚のみ、あいだを開いて折り上げます。(裏も同様に)
Open out the top flap and fold over. Do the same on the other side.

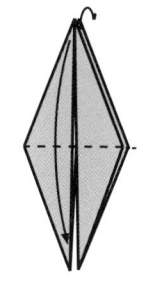

3. 上の1枚を折り下げます。(裏も同様に)
Fold the top flap down, and repeat on the other side.

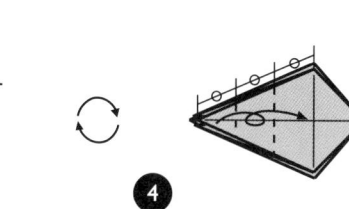

4. 上の1枚のみ、3等分にして巻くように折ります。
Fold the top flap over in three equal parts.

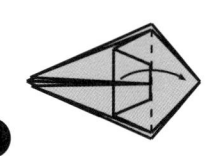

5. 図のように谷折り。
Make a valley fold as shown.

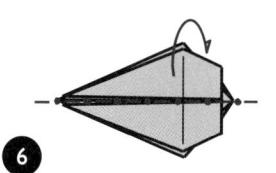

6. 全体を山折り。
Fold in half using a mountain fold.

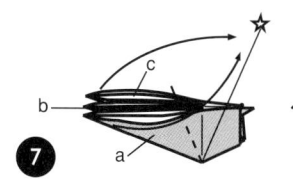

7. ☆の線に向って、外側のa、cのみ斜めに折ります。
Fold ⟨a⟩ and ⟨c⟩ back at an angle to meet along the line indicated by the star. Leave ⟨b⟩ as is.

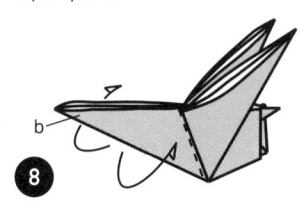

8. 残りのbを「かぶせ折り」(→p16)。
Fold ⟨b⟩ back using an outside reverse fold.

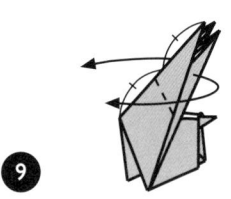

9. さらに「かぶせ折り」。
Then make another reverse fold as shown.

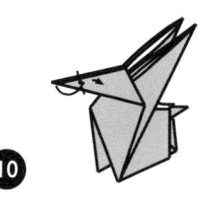

10. 鼻の先を内側へ折り込みます。
Fold the tip of the nose in.

11. 耳の外側の袋を開きます。
Open out the outside pocket on the ears.

12. できあがり
Finished!

★★ 〈豆干支〉寅 mini-tiger → 折り紙 p27

注 千代紙「花七宝」(黄)を使用。
裏の点線で切ってください。
Note: Use "Hana shippō" chiyogami paper (yellow).
Cut along the dotted line on the back.

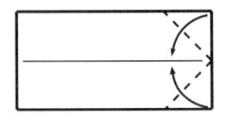

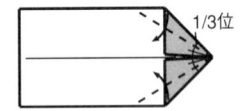

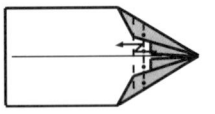

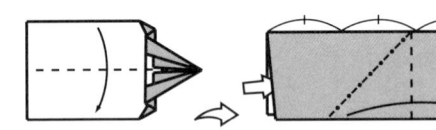

1
半分に折って折りすじを
つけ、角を2ヵ所折ります。
Fold in half to make a
crease, and then fold in
two corners as shown.

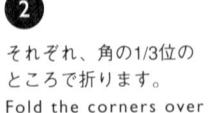

2
それぞれ、角の1/3位の
ところで折ります。
Fold the corners over
again, this time by 1/3.

3
図の位置で段折りします。
Make a stair fold as
shown.

4
全体を半分に谷折り。
Fold in half using a
valley fold.

5
図の位置で折りすじをつけて、あいだ
を開いて右に倒してたたみます。
Make a crease as shown, then
open out and fold over to the
right.

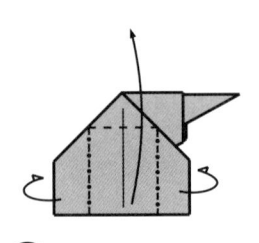

6
両側を山折りしながら、上
に折り上げます。
Fold upwards making a
mountain fold on each
side.

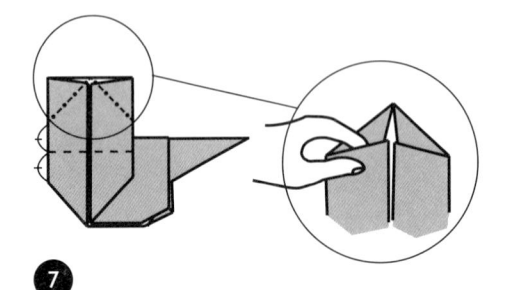

7
○の中は、「中割り折り」(→p16)で
中に折り込み、図の位置で谷折り。
In the circled section, fold
inwards using inside reverse folds,
and then make a valley fold as
shown.

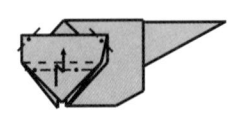

8
折ったところ。
角を少し折ってから、
2枚重ねて段折り。
Fold the corners over
slightly, and then make a
step fold with both
sheets together as
shown.

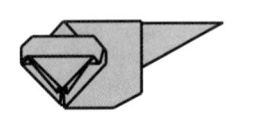

9
できあがり
Finished!

★〈豆干支〉卯 mini-rabbit → 折り紙 p27

注 千代紙「牡丹蝶」（白）を使用。裏の点線で切ってください。2匹のうさぎができます。
Note: Use "Botan chō" chiyogami paper (white). Cut along the dotted line on the back to make two rabbits.

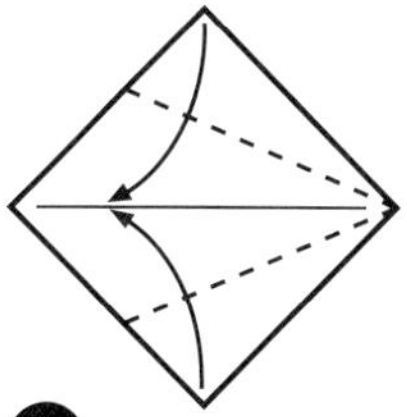

1
三角に折って折りすじをつけて、それにあうように折ります。
Fold over to form a triangle and make a crease, and then fold each side over so the edges meet in the center.

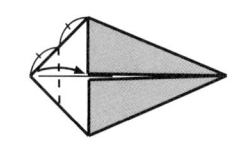

2
半分のところで、折ります。
Fold the flap over by half.

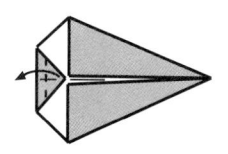

3
先端が少しはみ出るように谷折り。
Fold back over so the tip protrudes slightly.

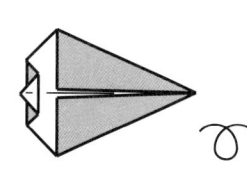

4
折ったところ。
This is how it should look.

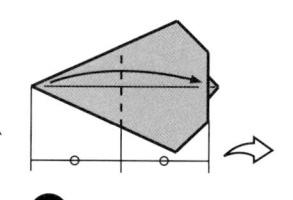

5
図の位置で折ります。
Fold over as shown.

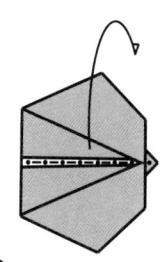

6
全体を半分に山折り。
Fold in half using a mountain fold.

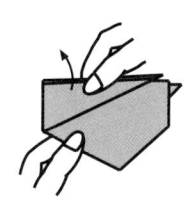

7
耳を少し引き上げます。
Pull the ears up slightly.

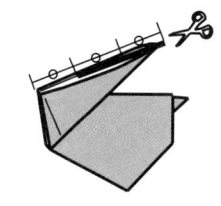

8
耳の先から2/3位まで切り込みを入れます。
From the tip of the ears, make a cut along 2/3 of their length as shown.

9
耳を少し開きます。
Open out the ears slightly.

10
できあがり
Finished!

✱✱ 巳 Snake → 折り紙 p31

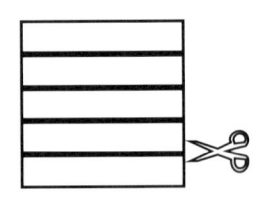

1
紙の裏の線にあわせて、5等分に切ります。
Cut the paper into five equal strips following the lines on the back of the paper.

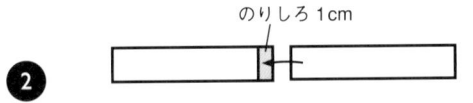

2
のりしろ1cm
のりしろを1cmずつ取って5枚を貼り合わせます。
Apply glue to 1cm at one tip of each strip, and stick the strips end-to-end.

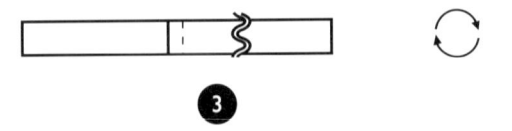

3
5枚貼り合わせたところ。
Turn round.

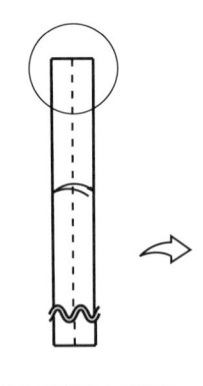

4
縦半分に折りすじをつけます。
Fold in half lengthwise to make a crease as shown.

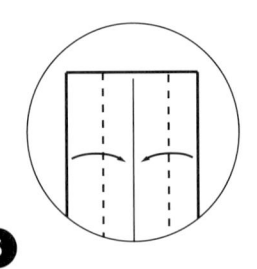

5
中央の線にあわせて両側を折ります。
Fold in each edge to meet at the center crease.

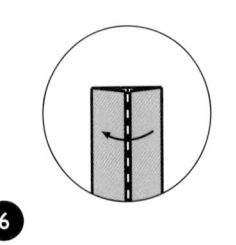

6
半分に折ります。
Fold in half.

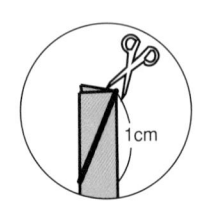

7
1cm
図の位置でまとめて切り落とし、開きます。
Make a diagonal cut as shown, then open out.

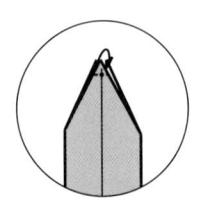

8
先端を1枚、少し山折り。
Make a mountain fold at the very tip of the top flap.

9
折ったところ。
Turn over.

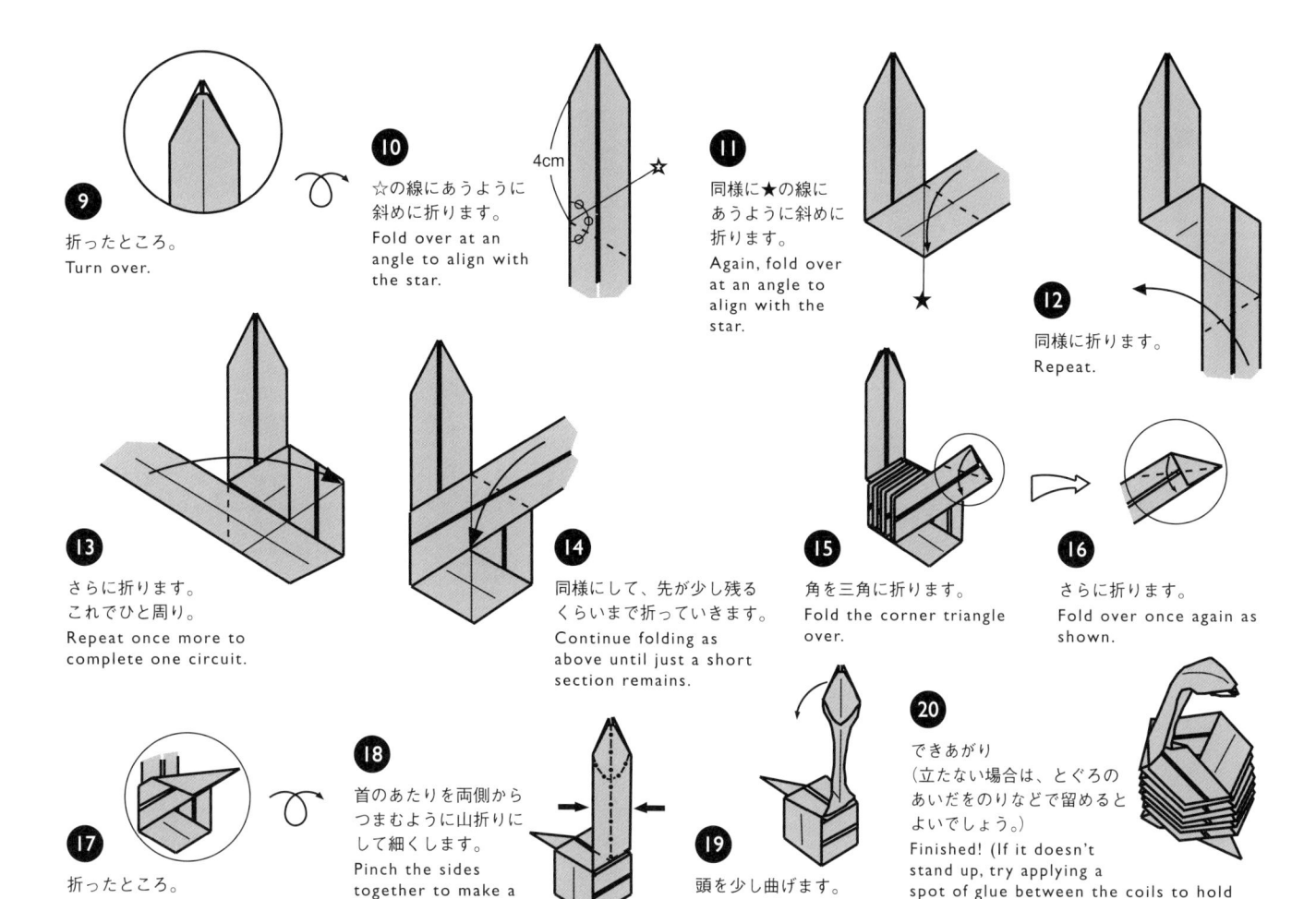

10
☆の線にあうように斜めに折ります。
Fold over at an angle to align with the star.

4cm

11
同様に★の線にあうように斜めに折ります。
Again, fold over at an angle to align with the star.

12
同様に折ります。
Repeat.

13
さらに折ります。
これでひと周り。
Repeat once more to complete one circuit.

14
同様にして、先が少し残るくらいまで折っていきます。
Continue folding as above until just a short section remains.

15
角を三角に折ります。
Fold the corner triangle over.

16
さらに折ります。
Fold over once again as shown.

17
折ったところ。
Turn over.

18
首のあたりを両側からつまむように山折りにして細くします。
Pinch the sides together to make a slimmer neck.

19
頭を少し曲げます。
Fold the head down.

20
できあがり
（立たない場合は、とぐろのあいだをのりなどで留めるとよいでしょう。）
Finished! (If it doesn't stand up, try applying a spot of glue between the coils to hold them in place.)

75

辰 Dragon → 折り紙 p29

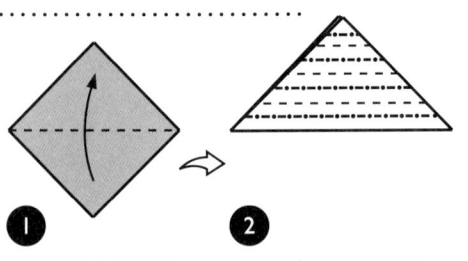

1 表を上にして三角に折ります。
Fold upwards to make a triangle.

2 8等分に折りすじをつけ、開きます。
Divide into eight equal parts and make creases, then open up.

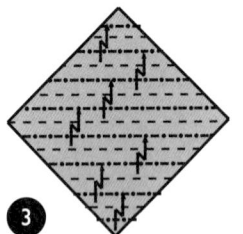

3 折り線を図のように直しながら、たたみます。
Using the creases, fold as shown.

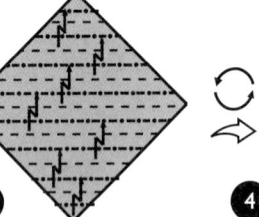

4 折ったところ。裏から半分のところで開きます。
Open out into two halves from behind.

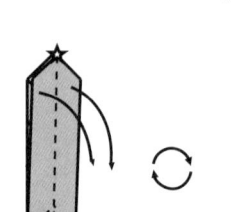

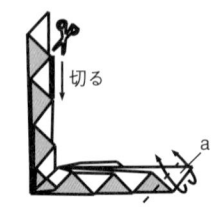

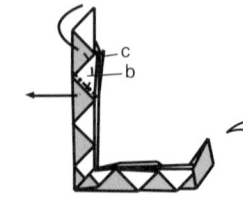

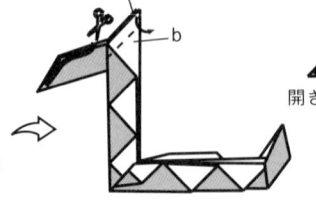

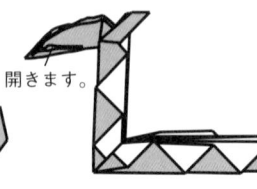

5 全体を半分に折ります。
Fold in half as shown.

6 上の1組にのみ折りすじをつけ、☆をつまんで全体を半分に折りながら下ろします。
Make creases in the top flap as shown, then pinch together the tip marked with a star and fold down.

7 図の位置で上の1枚のみ切り込みを入れます。(裏も同様に) aは「かぶせ折り」(→p16)
Make a cut in the upper flap as shown, and repeat on the other side. Then make an outside reverse fold at ‹a› as shown.

8 b、cを折らないようにして内側のみ「中割り折り」(→p16)。
Taking care not to fold ‹b› and ‹c›, make an inside reverse fold as shown.

9 b、cを折り、角を作ります。顔の上部に角の方から切り込みを入れ、ヒゲを作ります。
Fold ‹b› and ‹c› back as shown to make the horns. Make a wavy cut along the top of the face as shown to make the whiskers.

10 ヒゲを開いて、できあがり
Open out the whiskers. Finished!

★★ 〈豆干支〉辰 mini-dragon → 折り紙p33

注 千代紙「亀甲花菱」(黒)を使用。
裏の点線で切ってください。2匹の龍ができます。
Note: Use "Kikkō Hanabishi" chiyogami paper (black). Cut along the dotted line on the back to make two dragons.

1 縦半分の折りすじをつけてから、図のように折りすじをつけ、「三角折り」(→p16)の要領で折ります。
Fold in half lengthwise to make a crease, and then add creases as shown before folding over to make a triangular box fold.

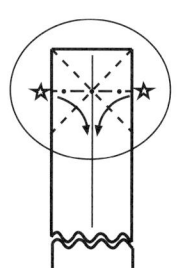

2 上の1組のみ谷折り。
Fold over the top flap as shown.

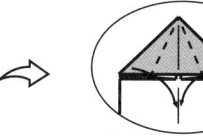

3 折ったところ。
Turn over.

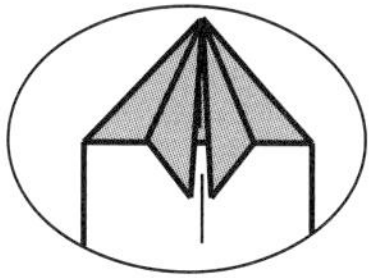

4 4つの角を谷折り。
Make valley folds on the corners as shown.

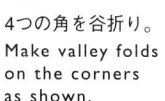

5 折ったところ。
Turn over.

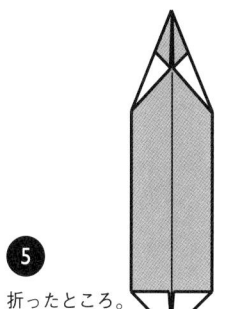

6 中央の線にあうように折ります。
Fold the edges in to meet at the center crease.

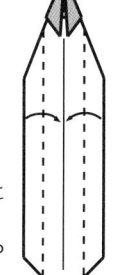

7 頭(上)の方から谷折り、山折りを繰り返してたたみます。
Fold the head over using a valley fold, then continue folding as shown and press down.

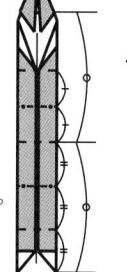

8 首部分を山折り (a、bは折りません)。
Make a mountain fold at the neck, without folding flaps ⟨a⟩ and ⟨b⟩.

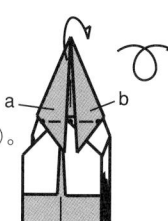

9 全体を山折り。
Fold in half using a mountain fold.

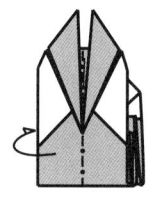

10 頭を横に引き出します。
Lift up the head.

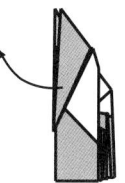

11 たたんだ部分を引き出しながら、形を整えます。
Pull out the tail, and press the body into shape as shown.

12 できあがり
Finished!

77

★ 〈豆干支〉巳 mini-snake → 折り紙 p33

注 千代紙「立涌」(赤)を使用。裏の点線で切ってください。2匹の蛇ができます。

Note: Use "Tatewaku" chiyogami paper (red). Cut along the dotted line on the back to make two snakes.

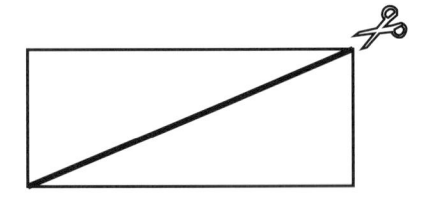

1
三角に切ります。
Cut along the diagonal as shown.

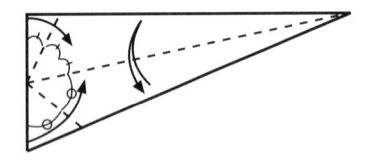

2
半分の折りすじをつけてから、角を図の位置で折ります。
Fold in half to make a crease, and then fold in the corners as shown.

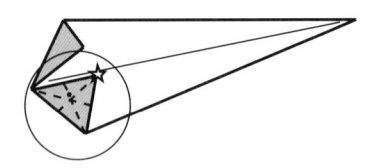

3
それぞれの角を半分に折って図のように折りすじをつけてから、☆をつまむようにしてたたみます。
Make creases as shown, and then pinch together to fold.

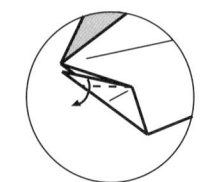

4
上の1組のみ谷折り。
Fold down the top flap at an angle.

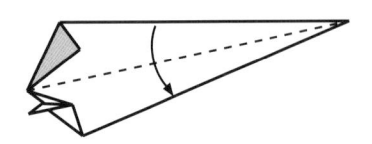

5
半分に折ります。
Fold in half.

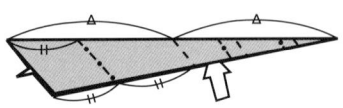

6
図のように折りすじをつけてから、あいだを開いて3ヵ所段折り。
Make creases and then fold using large stair folds.

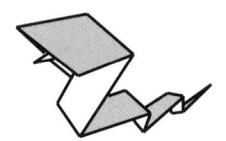

7
形を整えて、できあがり
Adjust the shape. Finished!

78

午 Horse → 折り紙 p35

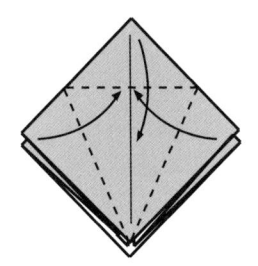

1
「四角折り」(→p16) をしてから、中央にあわせて図のようにまとめて折ります。
Make a square box fold, and then fold in the corners as shown.

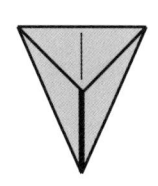

2
折ったところ。1の形に戻します。
Now unfold it again.

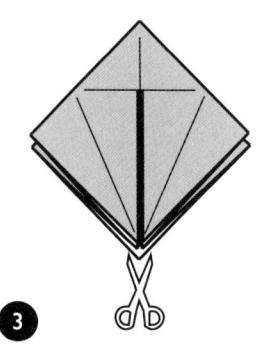

3
上の1枚のみ切り込みを入れます。(裏も同様に)
Cut the top flap as shown. Repeat on the other side.

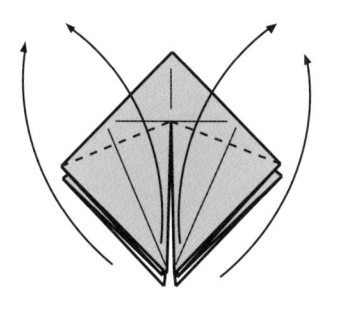

4
上の1枚をそれぞれ折り上げます。(裏も同様に)
Fold the top flaps up as shown. Repeat on the other side.

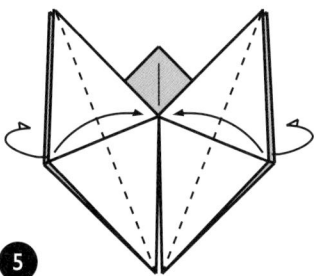

5
上の1枚をそれぞれ半分に折ります。(裏も同様に)
Fold the top flaps in half as shown. Repeat on the other side.

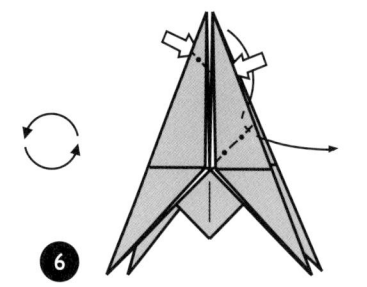

6
「中割り折り」(→p16) で、頭と尾を作ります。
Use inside reverse folds to make the head and tail.

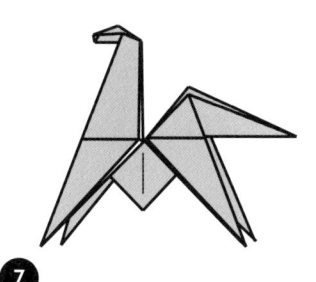

7
鼻先を折り込んで、できあがり
Fold the tip of the nose in. Finished!

★★★ 未 Sheep → 折り紙 p37

注 千代紙を裏の点線で4等分に切り、それぞれ頭と体を折ってください。2頭のひつじができます。
Note: Cut the paper into four equal parts along the dotted lines and make two sheep using one sheet each for the heads and bodies.

頭 Head

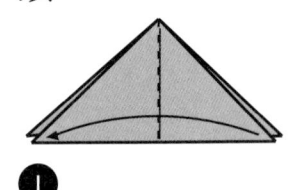

1
「三角折り」（→p16）をしてから、全体を半分に折ります。
Make a triangular box fold, and then fold in half.

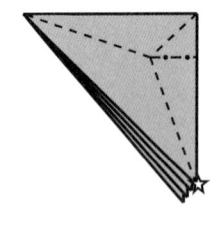

2
上の1組のみ、それぞれの角を半分に折って折りすじをつけ、☆をつまむようにして右側にたたみます。（裏も同様に）
Make creases on the top flap as shown, then fold pinching the sides together at the star. Repeat on the other side.

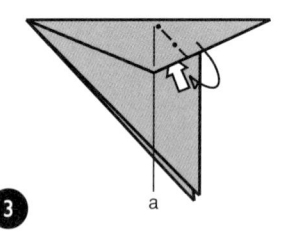

3
折ったところ。aの線にあうよう山折りして、角を作る。（裏も同様に）
Make a mountain fold to align with ‹a› for the horn. Repeat on the other side.

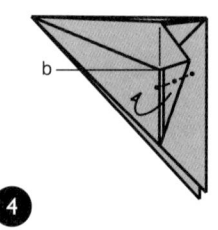

4
bの線にあうよう山折り。（裏も同様に）
Make a mountain fold to align with ‹b›. Repeat on the other side.

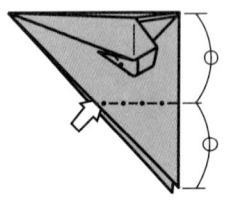

5
角の先をさらに山折り。半分のところで内側に折り込みます。（裏も同様に）
Make one more mountain fold to complete the horns. At the halfway point, fold the flaps inwards as shown.

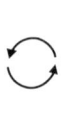

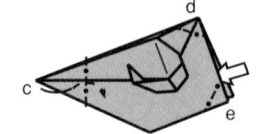

6
c、dは「中割り折り」（→p16）。eは山折りで内側に入れます。（裏も同様に）
Make inside reverse folds at ‹c› and ‹d›, and tuck in ‹e› using a mountain fold. Repeat on the other side.

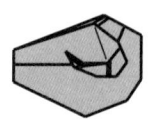

7
頭のできあがり
That's the head done!

80

体 Body

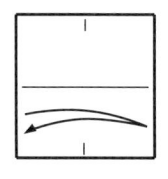

原案｜中島 進

1. 横半分に折りすじをつけてから、縦半分のところに印をつけます。
Fold in half to make a crease, and then make a mark at the halfway point.

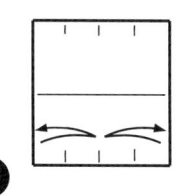

2. 1/4のところに印をつけます。
Make a mark at the quarter points.

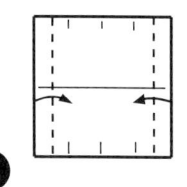

3. 1/8のところで谷折り。
Fold in 1/8 on each edge using a valley fold.

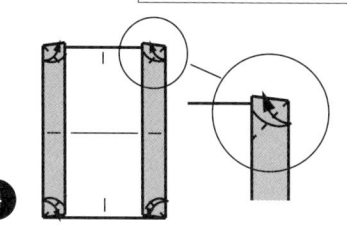

4. 4ヵ所を三角に折り、折りすじをつけます。
Make creases in each corner as shown.

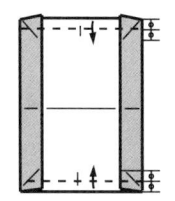

5. 4でつけた折りすじの半分の位置で谷折り。
Fold in the edges using a valley fold at halfway to the creases made in step 4.

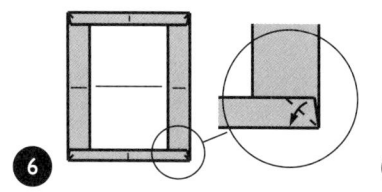

6. 4ヵ所を三角に谷折り。
Fold down the corner flaps as shown.

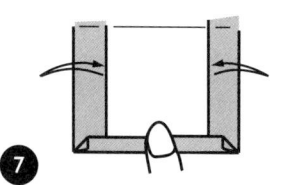

7. 下を押さえたまま、左右の紙を外側に開いて引き出し、もとに戻して脚を作ります。（上側も同様に）
Holding down as shown, lightly pull out the side flaps to make the feet. Repeat on the top.

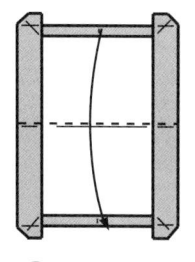

8. 半分に折ります。
Fold in half.

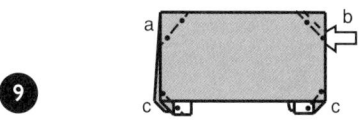

9. aは「中割り折り」（→p16）、bはあいだを開いて段折り。
Make an inside reverse fold at ‹a›, and a stair fold at ‹b›.

cはそれぞれ内側に山折り。（裏も同様に）
Then fold in on each side at ‹c›. Repeat on the other side.

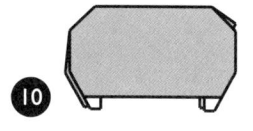

10. 体のできあがり
That's the body done!

11. 頭に体を挟んでのり付けして、できあがり
Insert the flaps on the body into the head. Finished!

★★★ 〈豆干支〉午 mini-horse → 折り紙 p39

注 千代紙「七宝花菱」(左)を使用。裏の点線で切ってください。2頭の馬ができます。

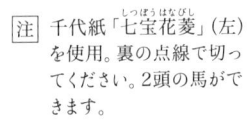

Note: Use "Shippō Hanabishi" chiyogami paper. Cut along the dotted line on the back to make two horses.

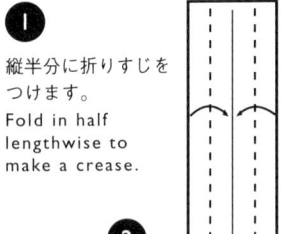

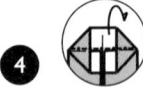

1 縦半分に折りすじをつけます。
Fold in half lengthwise to make a crease.

2 中央の線にあうように両側を折ります。
Fold the edges in to meet at the center crease.

3 0.5cm位のところに谷折りの折りすじをつけてから、あいだをつぶして開きます。
Make valley folds at 0.5cm to make creases each side, and then open out and flatten.

4 真ん中で山折り。
Make a mountain fold as shown.

5 折ったところ。
This is how it should look.

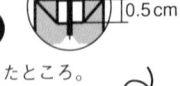

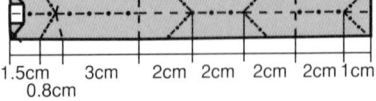

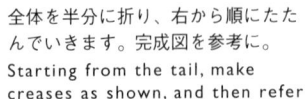

6 全体を半分に折り、右から順にたたんでいきます。完成図を参考に。
Starting from the tail, make creases as shown, and then refer to step 8 to fold into shape.

1.5cm　0.8cm　3cm　2cm　2cm　2cm　2cm　1cm

7 折ったところ。上の1組に切り込みを入れ、上に折り耳を作ります。(裏も同様に)
Make a cut as shown and fold up to make the ear. Repeat on the other side.

8 できあがり
Finished!

★ 〈豆干支〉未 mini-sheep → 折り紙 p39

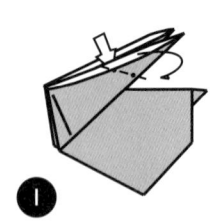

注 千代紙「観世水」(右)を使用。裏の点線で切ってください。2頭のひつじができます。

Note: Use "Kanze Mizu" chiyogami paper. Cut along the dotted line on the back to make two sheep.

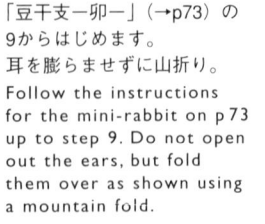

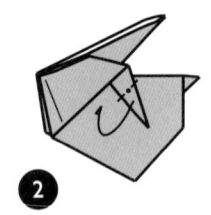

1 「豆干支—卯—」(→p73) の9からはじめます。耳を膨らませずに山折り。
Follow the instructions for the mini-rabbit on p73 up to step 9. Do not open out the ears, but fold them over as shown using a mountain fold.

2 もう1度山折り。
Make another mountain fold.

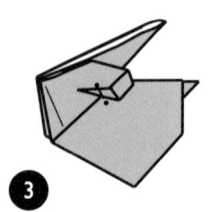

3 さらに山折り。反対側も1〜3までと同様にします。
Make one more mountain fold. Repeat steps 1–3 on the other side.

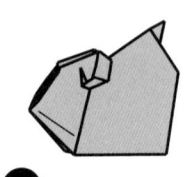

4 できあがり
Finished!

申 Monkey → 折り紙 p41

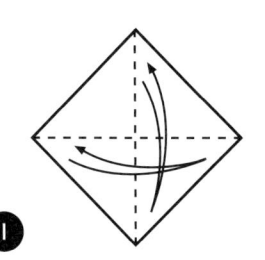

1. 折りすじをつけます。
Make creases as shown.

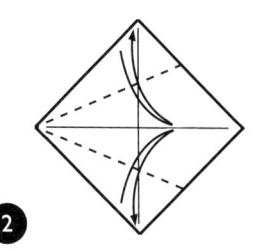

2. 中央の線にあうように折りすじをつけます。
Using the center lines as a guide, make two further creases.

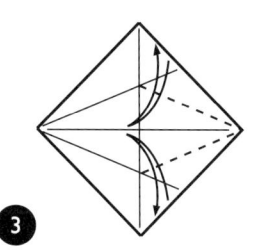

3. 図の位置まで折りすじをつけます。
Make two more creases as shown.

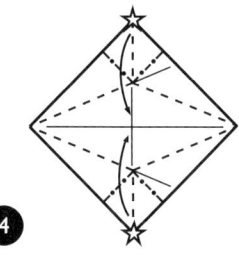

4. ☆をつまんで、折りすじ通りに真ん中に寄せながら折りたたみます。
Pinch the corners at the two stars as shown and fold towards the center along the creases, and then fold the flaps over.

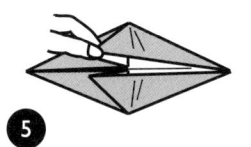

5. 折っているところ。
This is how it should look at this stage.

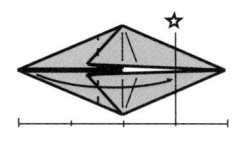

6. ☆の線にあうように谷折り。
Fold the tip over in a valley fold to align with the star.

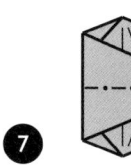

7. 全体を山折り。
Fold in half using a mountain fold.

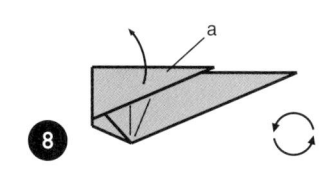

8. aを引き上げます。
Pull out the flap marked ⟨a⟩.

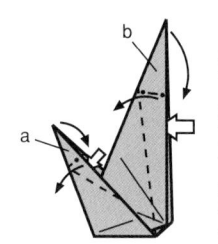

9. a、bともに、あいだを開いて折り、先端を上からつぶして頭を作ります。
For both ⟨a⟩ and ⟨b⟩, fold the tip down and open out flat as shown.

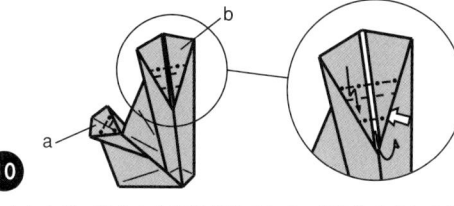

10. a、bともに、図のように段折りをして、顔の先を少し山折り。
For both ⟨a⟩ and ⟨b⟩, make a stair fold as shown, and finish off with a final mountain fold.

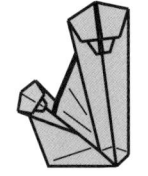

11. できあがり
Finished!

酉 Rooster → 折り紙 p43

中心 中心 — a

1 半分に折ります。
Fold in half.

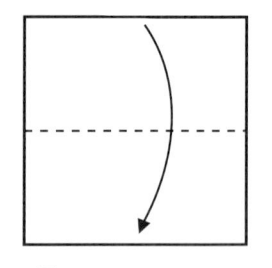

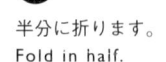

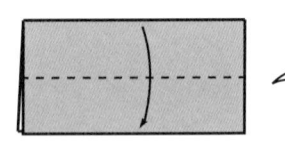

2 まとめて、半分に折ります。
Fold in half once again.

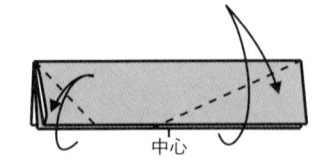

3 まとめて、図のように折って折りすじをつけます。
Fold as shown to make creases.

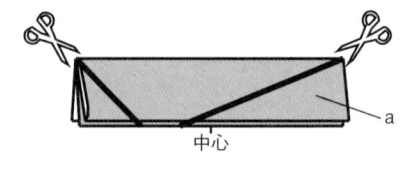

4 3でつけた折りすじ通りにまとめて切り取ります。(aは、後で使います。)
Cut along the creases made in step 3. The pieces marked ⟨a⟩ will be used later.

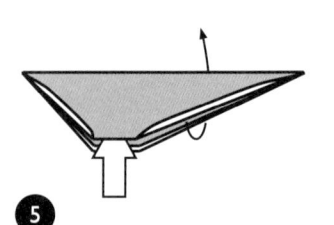

5 あいだを開いて後ろを上げます。
Open out flat.

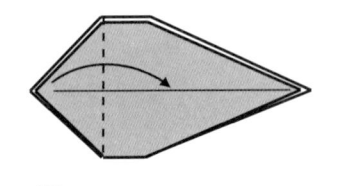

6 図のように折ります。
Fold over as shown.

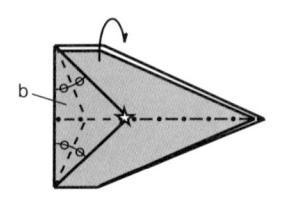

7 ☆をつまんで、bの部分を図のように谷折りしてから、全体を山折りします。
Pinching the star, form valley folds on ⟨b⟩ as shown, while folding in half lengthwise using a mountain fold.

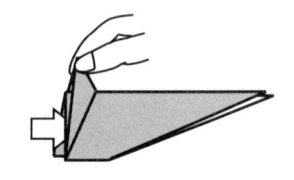

8 折ったところ。あいだを開きます。
Open out the back flap.

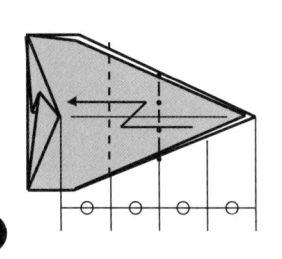

9
図の位置で、全体を段折りします。
Make stair folds as shown.

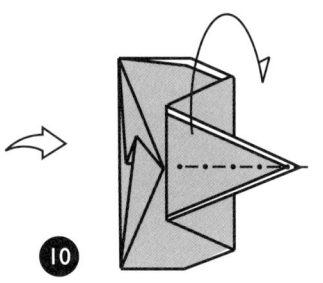

10
全体を半分に山折りします。
Fold in half using a mountain fold.

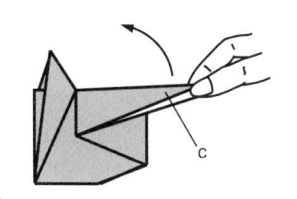

11
cを2枚一緒に引き上げます。
Pull ⟨c⟩ up as shown.

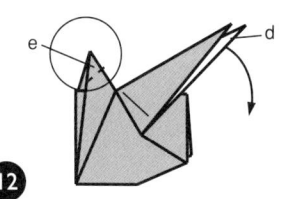

12
dは、少し下に引き下げます。
eの部分は、13〜15の拡大図を参照。
Pull ⟨d⟩ down slightly. For ⟨e⟩, follow steps 13–15.

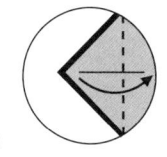

13
(eを開いて真上から見た拡大図)
上の1枚のみ半分位に折ります。
(Close-up of ⟨e⟩ straight on)
Fold the top flap back as shown.

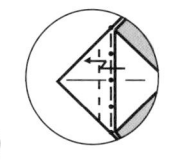

14
下の1枚を段折りします。
Make a stair fold on the lower flap.

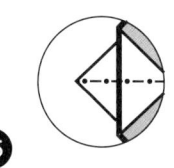

15
山折りして16の形にします。
Use a mountain fold on both flaps to achieve the image shown in step 16.

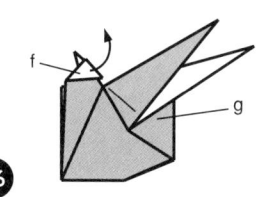

16
fを引き上げ18のようにする。
Pull up ⟨f⟩.

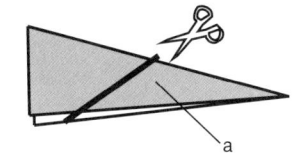

17
4で切り落とした三角のうち、内側の大きな1枚を図のように切り取ります (a)。
16のgにaを貼ります。
Take the larger inside piece cut from ⟨a⟩ in step 4, and stick onto ⟨g⟩ in step 16.

18
内側に山折りします。
(裏も同様に)
Fold in the top flap as shown using a mountain fold. Repeat on the other side.

19
できあがり
Finished!

★★★

〈豆干支〉申 mini-monkey → 折り紙 p45

注 千代紙「蝶」(ちょう)(白)を使用。
裏の点線で切ってください。
Note: Use the "Chō" chiyogami paper (white).
Cut along the dotted line on the back.

原案 | 中島 進

1 半分で折りすじをつけてから、図のように折ります。
Make a center crease, and then fold the corners as shown.

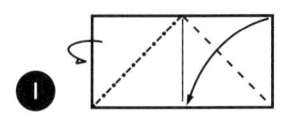

2 2枚一緒に、図の位置で折りすじをつけます。
Keeping both sheets together, make a crease as shown.

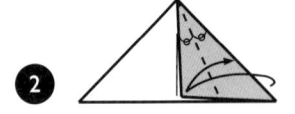

3 2枚一緒に折りすじをつけます。
Make another crease.

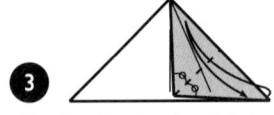

4 ★をつまむようにして、同様に折りすじをつけます。a側も2～4と同様にします。
Pinching the corner marked with a star, make another crease as shown. Repeat steps 2-4 on side 〈a〉.

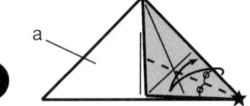

5 ☆と☆を水平に結んだ線あたりまで、切り込みを入れます。
Make a cut from the tip down to a line level with the stars.

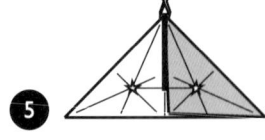

6 2枚一緒に折りすじどおりにたたみながら、★をつまんで折り上げます。(左も同様に)
Folding along the creases as shown, pinch together at the star and pull up.

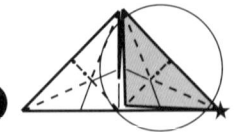

7 途中図
This is how it should look partway.

8 折ったところ。それぞれ、上の1組のあいだを開いて折ります。
Repeat on the other side. Now fold over the top flap on each side as shown.

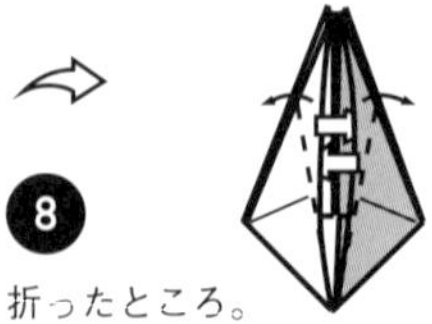

9 先端を谷折りしてつぶし、顔を作ります。
Fold over the tips using valley folds, and flatten for the faces.

10 図のように段折りをして、顔の先を少し山折り。
Make stair folds as shown, and tuck the chin under with a mountain fold.

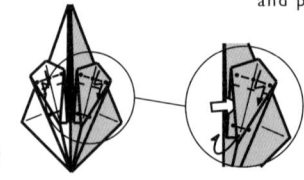

11 折りすじをつけます。
Make a crease.

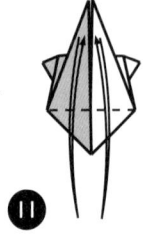

12 b、cは2～4、6と同じ要領で折り、尾を作ります。
dは図のように谷折り。
Fold 〈b〉 and 〈c〉 following steps 2-4 and 6 for the tails. Fold 〈d〉 using a valley fold as shown.

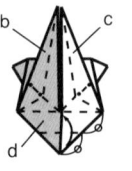

13  尾を少し丸めて、できあがり
Twist the tails around a little. Finished!

86

★
〈豆干支〉酉 mini-rooster → 折り紙 p45

注 千代紙「翁格子」（黄）を使用。裏の点線で切ってください。2羽の鶏ができます。
Note: Use "Okina Gōshi" chiyogami paper (yellow). Cut along the dotted line on the back to make two roosters.

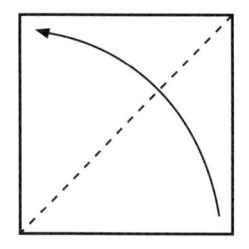

1
三角に折ります。
Fold over to make a triangle.

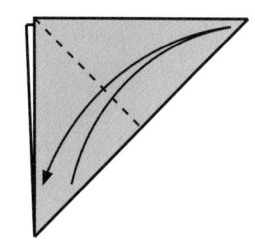

2
折りすじをつけます。
Make a crease.

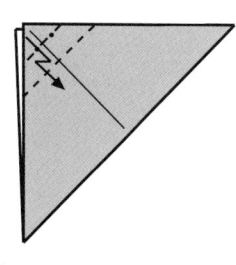

3
上の1枚のみ段折りをします。
Make a stair fold on the top flap only.

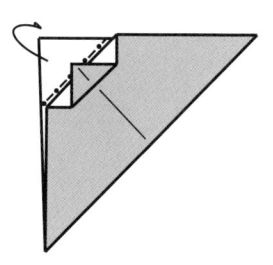

4
3で折ったところにあわせて、後ろの1枚を山折り。
Fold the back flap using a mountain fold, following the line of the fold made in step 3.

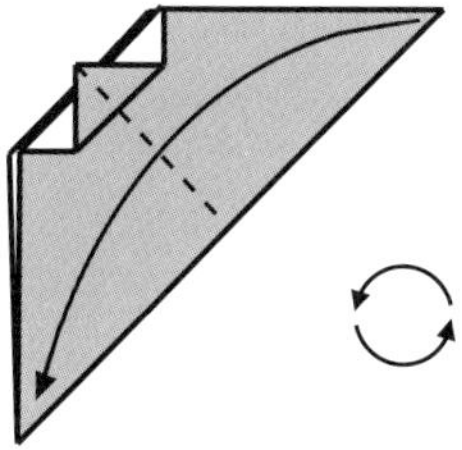

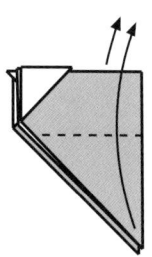

5
全体を半分に折ります。
Fold in half as shown.

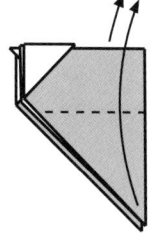

6
図のように上に向って折ります。（裏も同様に）
Fold the flaps on either side up as shown.

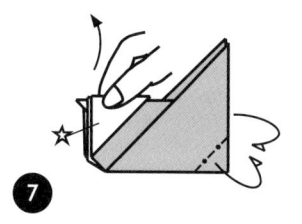

7
☆をつまんで斜めに引き上げます。下の角は内側に折り込みます。（裏も同様に）
Pinch together at the star, and pull up at an angle. Fold the bottom corner in as shown, and repeat on the other side.

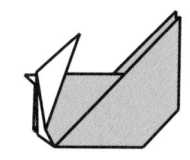

8
できあがり
Finished!

戌 Dog → 折り紙 p47

原案 | Paul Jackson

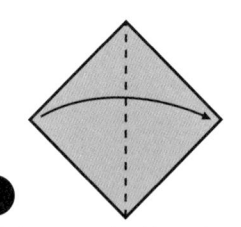

1
表を上にして三角に折ります。
Place the paper colored surface up, and fold over to form a triangle.

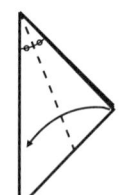

2
上の1枚のみ谷折り。(裏も同様に)
Fold the top flap over using a valley fold. Repeat on the other side.

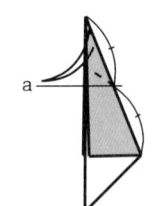

3
aの線にあうように斜めに折りすじをつけ、開きます。
Fold over to align with ⟨a⟩, and make a crease. Open out.

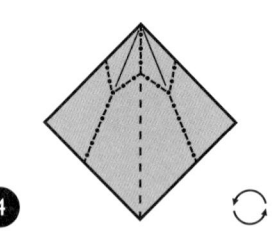

4
折りすじを図のように直して、5のようにたたみます。
Fold along the creases as shown.

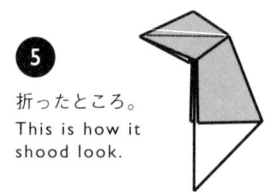

5
折ったところ。
This is how it shood look.

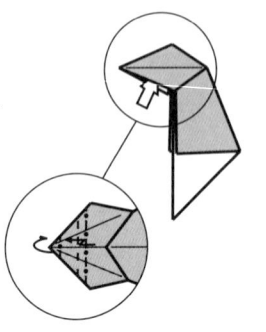

6
頭を開いてから、段折りして顔をつくり、鼻先を内側に折ります。
Open out the head, and make a stair fold for the face, then fold the tip of the nose under.

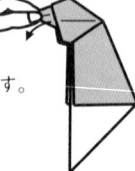

7
鼻を少し下向きにします。
Pull the nose down slightly at an angle.

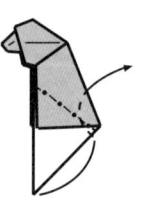

8
内側の紙を「中割り折り」(→p16)。
Pull up the inside flap in an inside reverse fold.

9
あいだを開いて段折り。
Open out and make a stair fold.

10
できあがり
Finished!

88

亥 Boar → 折り紙 p49

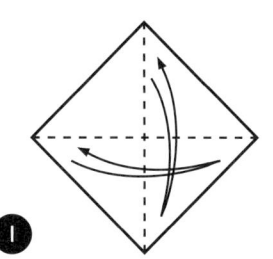

原案 | 辻 昭雄

1. 折りすじをつけます。
Make creases.

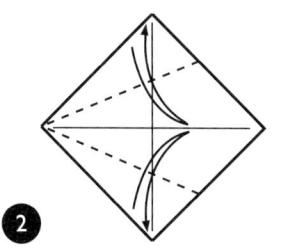

2. 中央の線にあうように折りすじをつけます。
Fold the edges into the center and make creases.

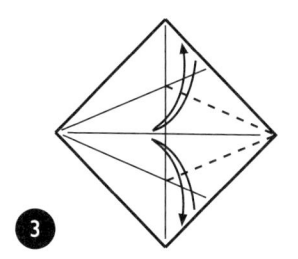

3. 図の位置まで折りすじをつけます。
Do the same on the other side, and make creases as shown.

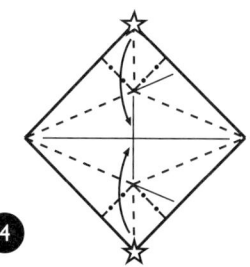

4. ☆をつまんで、折りすじ通りに真ん中に寄せながら折りたたみます。
Pinch together at the stars, and fold in along the creases.

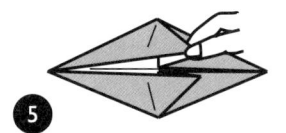

5. 折っているところ。
This is how it should look.

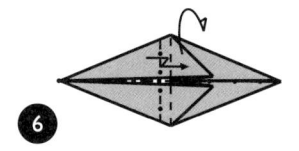

6. 真ん中で段折りし、全体を山折り。
Make a stair fold in the middle, and then fold over using a mountain fold.

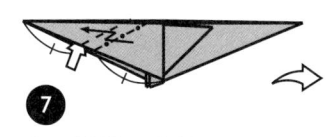

7. あいだを開いて段折り。
Open out and make a stair fold.

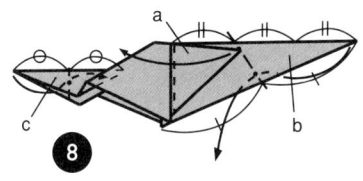

8. aは谷折り。（裏も同様に）
b、cは「中割り折り」（→p16）。
Fold over ⟨a⟩ using a valley fold, and repeat on the other side. Make inside reverse folds at ⟨b⟩ and ⟨c⟩ as shown.

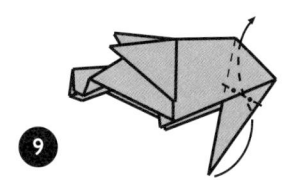

9. 「中割り折り」でしっぽを作ります。
Make another inside reverse fold for the tail.

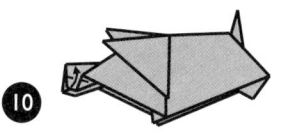

10. 鼻先を谷折り。（裏も同様に）
Fold the tips of the nose using valley folds as shown.

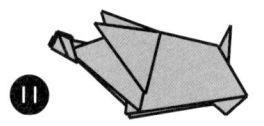

11. できあがり
Finished!

★★★ 〈豆干支〉戌 mini-dog → 折り紙 p51

注 千代紙「豆絞り」(白)を使用。裏の点線で切ってください。2匹の犬ができます。
Note: Use "Mameshibori" chiyogami paper (white). Cut along the dotted line on the back to make two dogs.

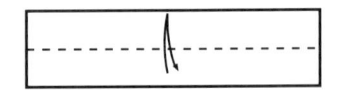

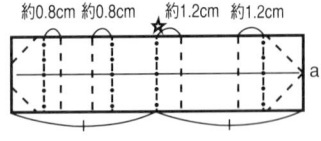

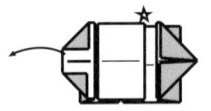

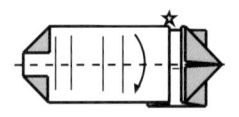

約0.8cm 約0.8cm 約1.2cm 約1.2cm

1
横半分の折り筋をつけます。
Fold in half lengthwise and make a crease.

2
aの方から、折りすじどおりに折っていきます。
Starting from ‹a›, make folds as shown.

3
折ったところ。
☆のところまで戻します。
This is what it should look like. Now unfold it as far as the star.

4
全体を半分に折ります。
Fold in half.

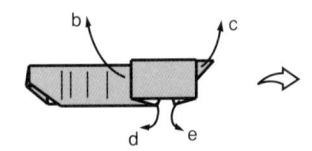

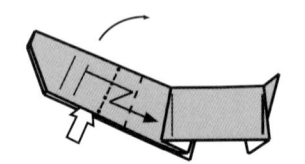

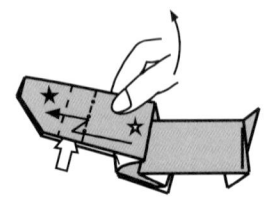

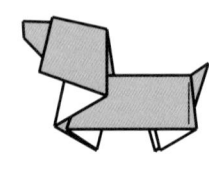

5
b、cを引き上げて、
d、eを少し出します。
Pull ‹b› and ‹c› up, and then pull ‹d› and ‹e› out.

6
あいだを開いて、
かぶせるように段折り。
Open out and make a stair fold so that it partially covers the body.

7
☆をつまんで引き上げてから、
★のあいだを開いて段折り。
Pull up at the white star, and then open out by the black star and make a stair fold.

8
できあがり
Finished!

90

★ 〈豆干支〉亥 mini-boar → 折り紙 p.51

注 千代紙「五崩し」(紫)を使用。
裏の点線で切ってください。
Note: Use "Gokuzushi" chiyogami paper (purple).
Cut along the dotted line on the back.

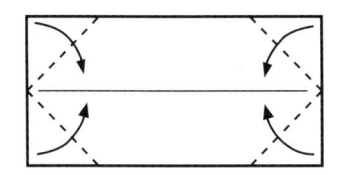

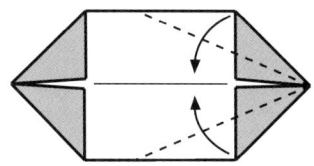

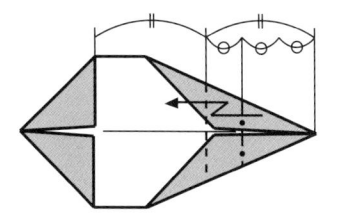

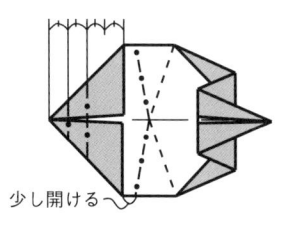

1
半分に折って折りすじをつけ、角を4ヵ所とも三角に折ります。
Fold in half lengthwise to make a crease, then fold the corners in as shown.

2
図のように中央の線にあうように折ります。
Fold over to the center line as shown.

3
図の位置で、段折り。
Make a stair fold as shown.

4
図の位置で、裏側へ2回山折りをして巻きます。中央に、折りすじをつけます。
Fold the tip over twice using mountain folds as shown. Make creases in the center.

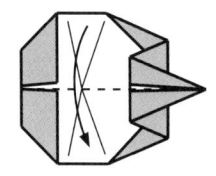

少し開ける

5
全体を半分に折ります。
Fold in half.

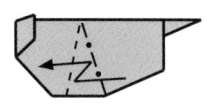

6
4でつけた折りすじを使って段折り。(裏も同様に)
Make a stair fold using the creases made in step 4. Repeat on the other side.

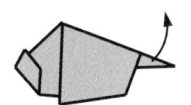

7
尾を引き上げます。
Pull the tail up.

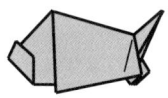

8
できあがり
Finished!

91

★のしつきご祝儀袋 Decorative envelope with a noshi decoration → 折り紙 p53

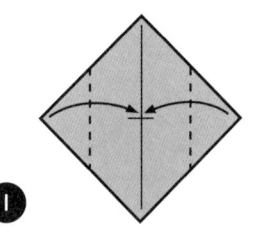

1
三角に折って折りすじをつけてから、中心に印をつけ、そこにあうように折ります。
Fold into a triangle and make a crease. Make a mark in the center, and then fold in the corners as shown.

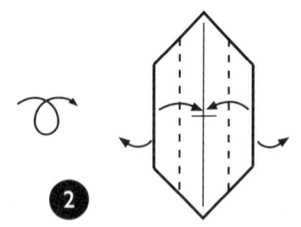

2
裏側の三角を引き出すようにしながら、谷折り。
Fold the edges into the center, and pull out the flaps from behind as shown.

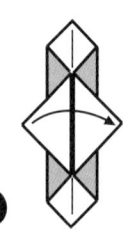

3
左側の三角を右に倒します。
Fold the left-hand flap over onto the right.

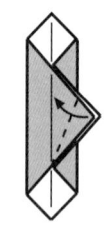

4
上の1枚のみ中央の線にあわせて折ります。
Fold the top flap over to line up with the center.

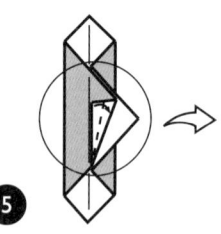

5
4で折ったところにあうように折ります。
Fold back over as shown to line up with the fold made in step 4.

6
まとめて中央の線で折ります。
Fold back along the center line.

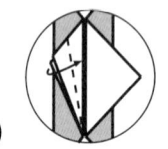

7
中央にあうように折ります。
Now fold over once more to line up with the center.

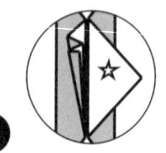

8
折ったところ。☆も4〜7と同様に折ります。
Repeat steps 4–7 on the other flap.

9
図のように三角に内側に折ります。
Fold the tip of the flaps in as shown.

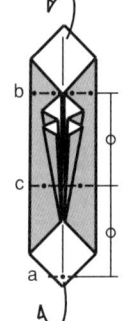

10
a、b、cの順に山折りします。
Fold ⟨a⟩, ⟨b⟩, and ⟨c⟩ over in that order using mountain folds.

11
10で折ったaがdにつくように、中に差し込みます。
Insert ⟨a⟩ from step 10 into ⟨d⟩ to secure.

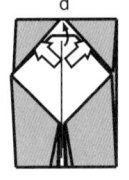

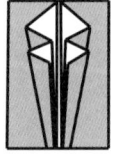

12
できあがり
Finished!

盃形のお年玉袋 Decorative cup-style envelope

→ 折り紙 p55

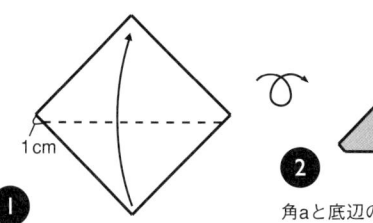

1 1cmずらして折ります。
Fold over 1cm from the center line.

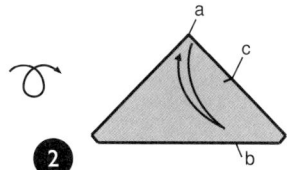

2 角aと底辺のbをあわせるようにして、cの位置を軽く折って印をつけます。
Fold corner ⟨a⟩ of the top flap down to point ⟨b⟩, and make a light mark at ⟨c⟩.

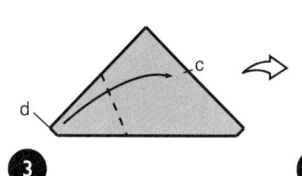

3 dがcにあうように折ります。
Fold corner ⟨d⟩ over to the mark at ⟨c⟩.

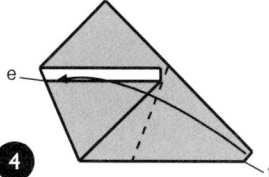

4 fがeにあうように、折ります。
Fold corner ⟨e⟩ over to point ⟨f⟩.

5 2枚一緒に差し込みます。
Fold both flaps over and insert as shown.

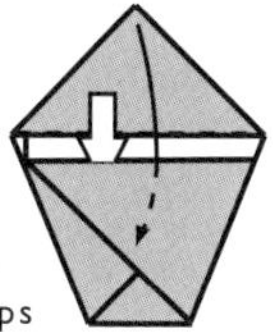

6 できあがり
Finished!

斜め帯のお年玉袋 Decorative envelope with a sash

→ 折り紙 p57

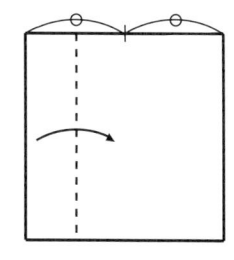

1 半分のところに印をつけ、そこにあうように折ります。
Make a mark at the center, and fold the edge over to line up with it.

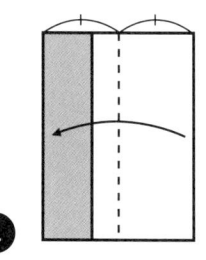

2 半分に折ります。
Fold in half as shown.

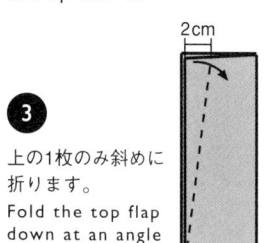

3 上の1枚のみ斜めに折ります。
Fold the top flap down at an angle as shown.

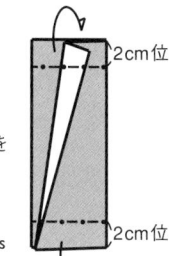

4 図の位置で上と下を山折り。
Make mountain folds at the top and bottom edges as shown.

5 できあがり
Finished!

十文字のポチ袋 Decorative envelope with a cross → 折り紙 p59

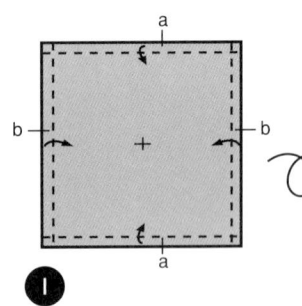

1. 中心に印をつけてから、4辺を1cmほどa、bの順に折ります。
Make a mark in the center of the paper, and then fold the edges marked ‹a› and ‹b› over by 1 cm in that order.

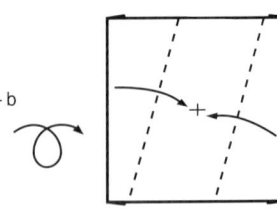

2. 中心にあわせて、両側を斜めに折ります。
Fold both sides over as shown so that they meet at the center mark.

3. 折ったところ。開きます。
This is what it should look like. Open out again.

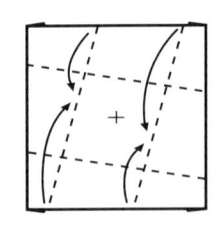

4. 2と同様に斜めに折ります。
Repeat step 2 as shown.

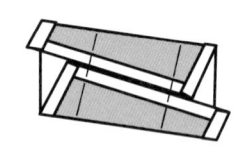

5. 折ったところ。開きます。
You should now have this. Open it out once more.

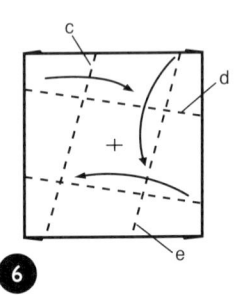

6. c、d、eの順に折っていきます。
Now fold over ‹c›, ‹d›, and ‹e› in that order.

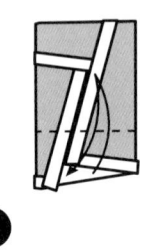

7. 折りすじをつけます。
Make a crease.

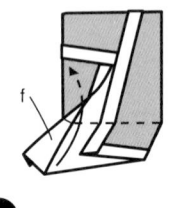

8. fを少し開いて中に入れ込み、たたみます。
Slightly open out at ‹f› and tuck in as shown.

9. できあがり
Finished!

94

★★ たとう折りのポチ袋 Tatō-ori pochibukuro

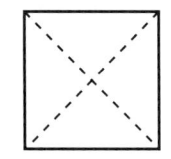

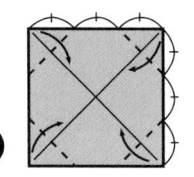

→ 折り紙 p61

1 折りすじをつけます。
Make creases.

2 図のように折ります。
Fold in the corners as shown.

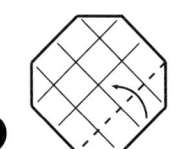

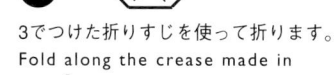

3 中心にあうように折りすじをつけます。
Fold the edges into the center line to make creases as shown.

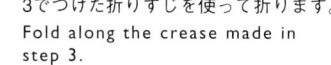

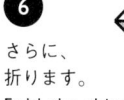

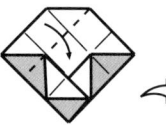

4 3でつけた折りすじを使って折ります。
Fold along the crease made in step 3.

5 4と同様に折ります。
Fold along the next crease, as in step 4.

6 さらに、折ります。
Fold the third edge down.

7 最初に折ったaを少し開いて、bの半分を中に入れ込み、たたみます。
Slightly open out the first fold made at ⟨a⟩, tuck in half of ⟨b⟩ and fold down.

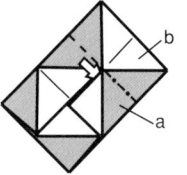

8 できあがり
Finished!

★ 伝承折りの手紙 Traditional origami letter

→ 折り紙 p63

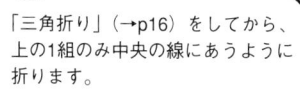

1 「三角折り」（→p16）をしてから、上の1組のみ中央の線にあうように折ります。
Make a triangular box fold, and then fold the top flap over on each side to align at the center.

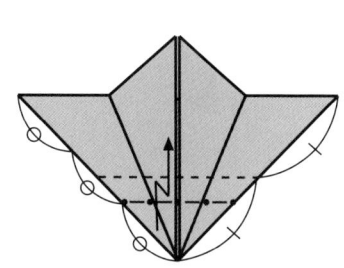

2 図のように段折り。
Make a stair fold as shown.

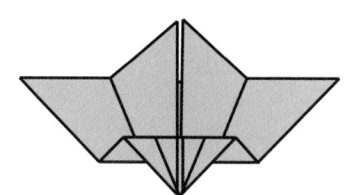

3 できあがり
Finished!

オリガミ様（小林一夫）

1941年東京・湯島に生まれる。1859年創業の和紙専門店「ゆしまの小林」四代目。おりがみ会館（お茶の水）館長。内閣府認証NPO法人国際おりがみ協会理事長。日本の「折る文化」「和紙文化」を国内外に伝えることをライフワークにしている。著書多数。

Mr. Origami (Kazuo Kobayashi)

Kazuo Kobayashi was born in Yushima, Tokyo in 1941, and is the fourth generation owner of the family-run Japanese paper specialty store "Yushima no Kobayashi" established in 1859. He is also the director of the Origami Center and the chief director of the International Origami Society, an NPO certified by the Japanese Cabinet Office. Mr. Origami, as he is known, has made it his lifework to promote what he calls the "Culture of folding paper" and the "Culture of Japanese paper" both in Japan and overseas, and has written many books on the subject.

主な参考文献／『日本の文様』（小林一夫著・日本ヴォーグ社）
『日本・中国の文様事典』（視覚デザイン研究所）
『日本の伝統文様事典』（講談社）
『江戸文様事典』（河出書房新社）
『日本文様事典』（河出書房新社）

おとなのORIGAMI-BOOK　オリガミ様のお江戸折り紙

十二支おりがみ

発行日　2008年11月7日　第1刷
　　　　2024年3月22日　第6刷

著　者　小林一夫
発行者　森田浩章
発行所　株式会社講談社
　　　　〒112-8001 東京都文京区音羽2-12-21
　　　　電話　編集　03-5395-3560
　　　　　　　販売　03-5395-4415
　　　　　　　業務　03-5395-3615

印刷所　NISSHA株式会社
製本所　大口製本印刷株式会社
©Kazuo Kobayashi 2008, Printed in Japan

定価はカバーに表示してあります。
落丁本・乱丁本は購入書店名を明記のうえ、小社業務宛にお送り下さい。送料小社負担にてお取り替えします。なお、この本についてのお問い合わせは、第一事業本部企画部からだとこころ編集宛にお願いいたします。本書のコピー、スキャン、デジタル化等の無断複製は著作権法上での例外を除き禁じられています。本書を代行業者等の第三者に依頼してスキャンやデジタル化することはたとえ個人や家庭内の利用でも著作権法違反です。

ISBN978-4-06-261763-5　N.D.C. 790　96p　15cm

KODANSHA

企画協力／「ゆしまの小林」お茶の水・おりがみ会館
　　　　　TEL 03-3811-4025／URL http://www.origamikaikan.co.jp/
編集協力／町田陽子、久保恵子
アートディレクション／坂川栄治
デザイン／田中久子、永井亜矢子
作品制作・折り図作成／湯浅信江
英訳／Ginny Tapley Takemori
英文校正／Haruko Horiuchi
イラスト／cochae
撮影／講談社写真部（渡辺充俊）